ILLUSTRIOUS butterflies

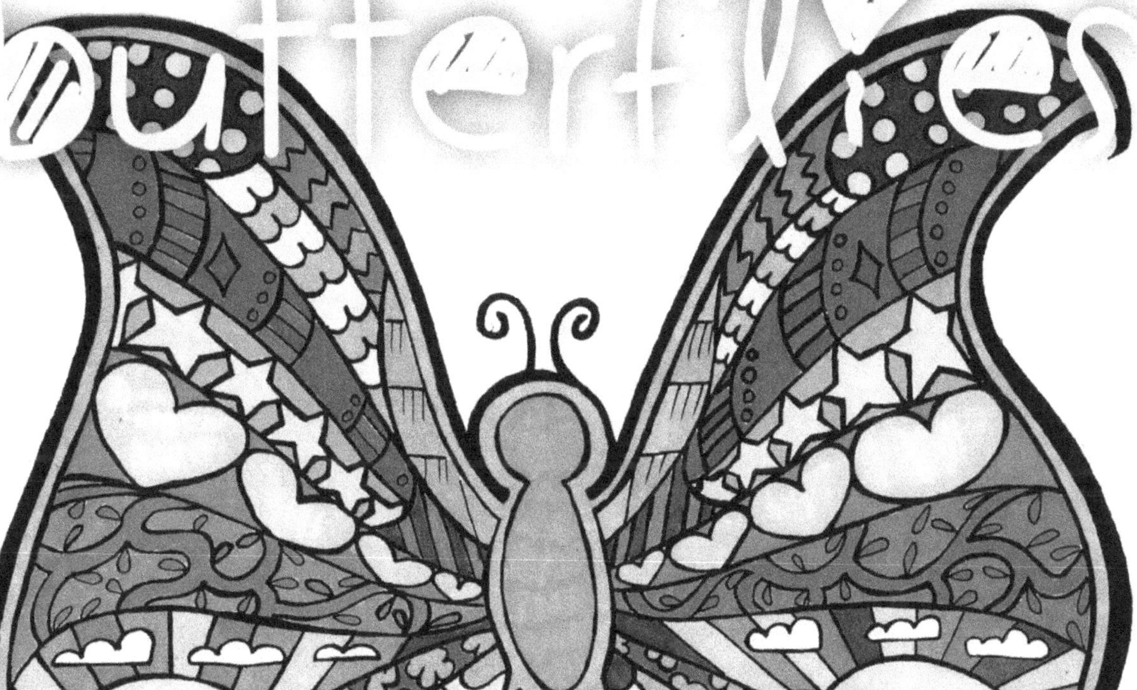

BY: AKEEM WAYNE

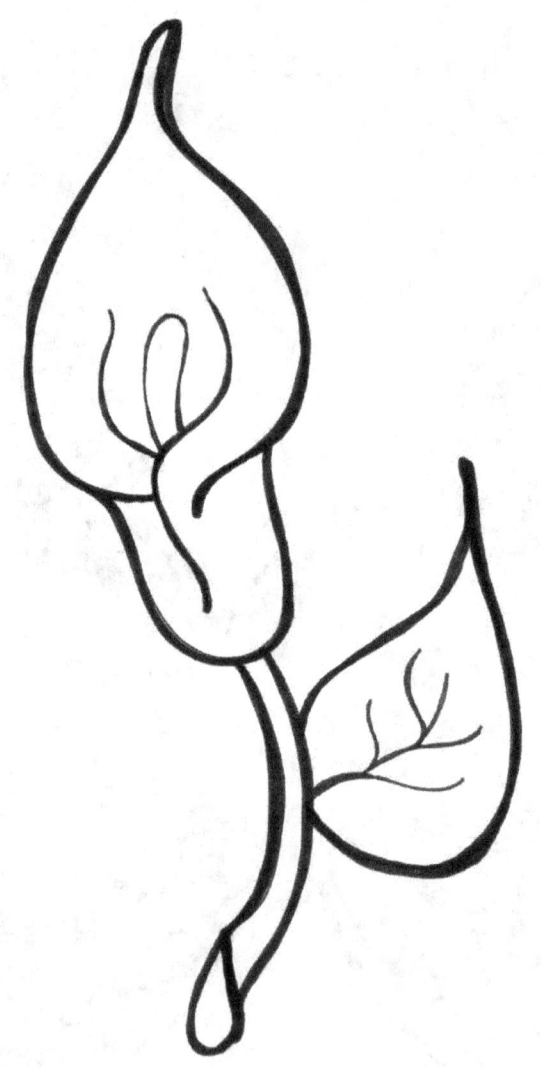

This Book Belongs to:

_____

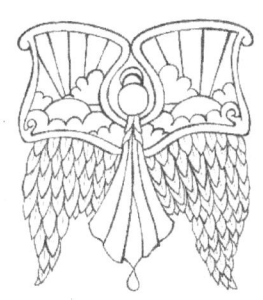

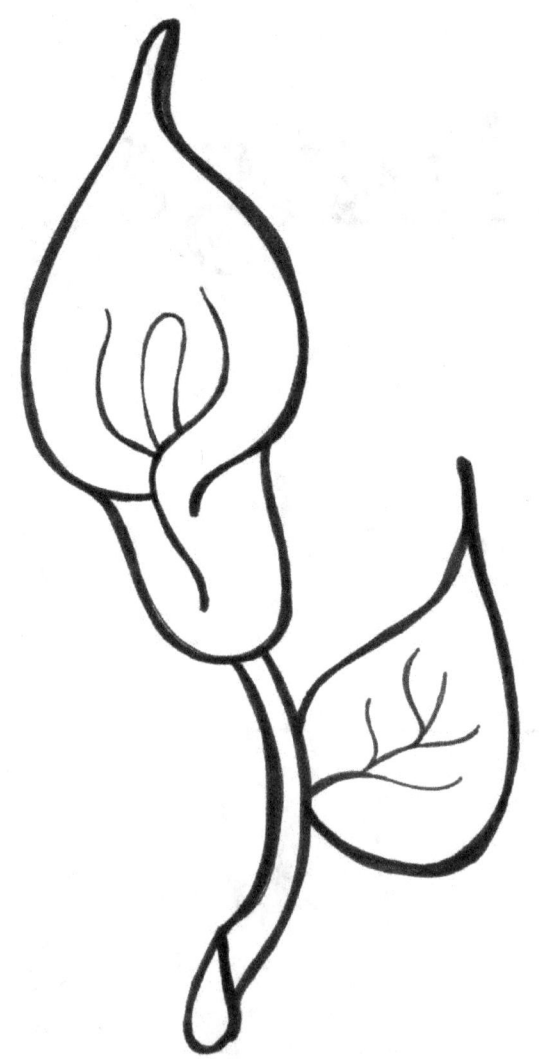

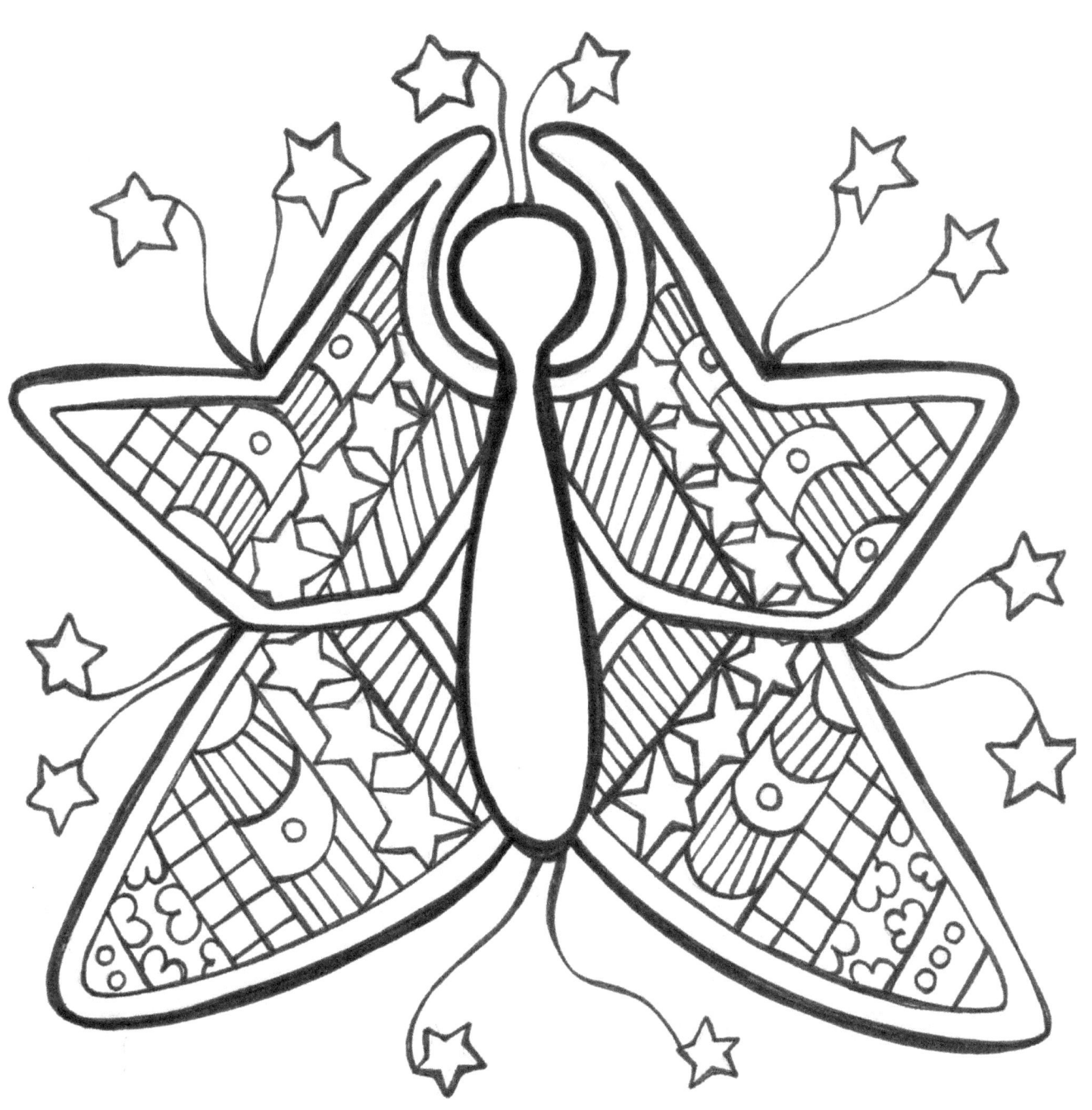

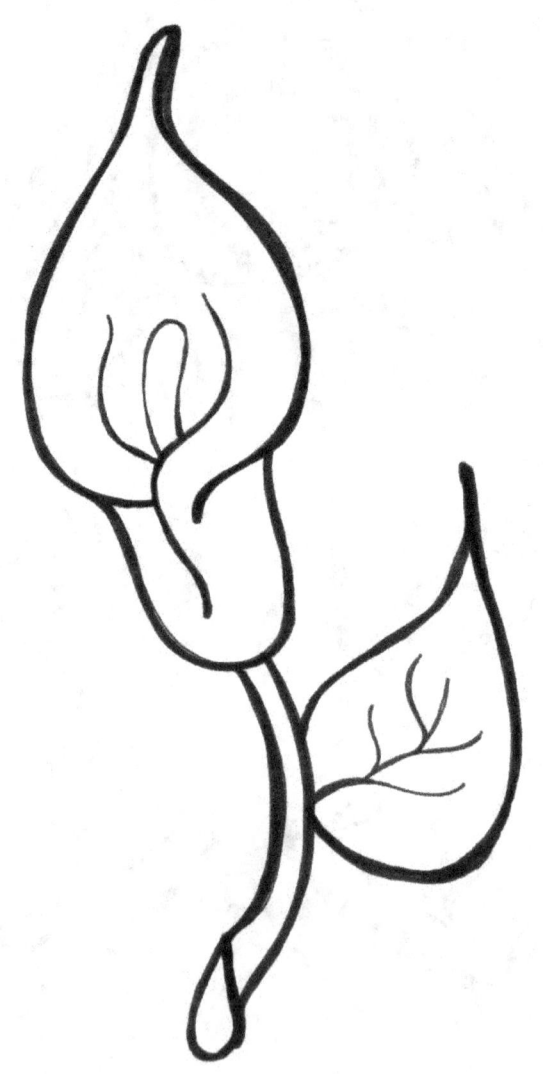

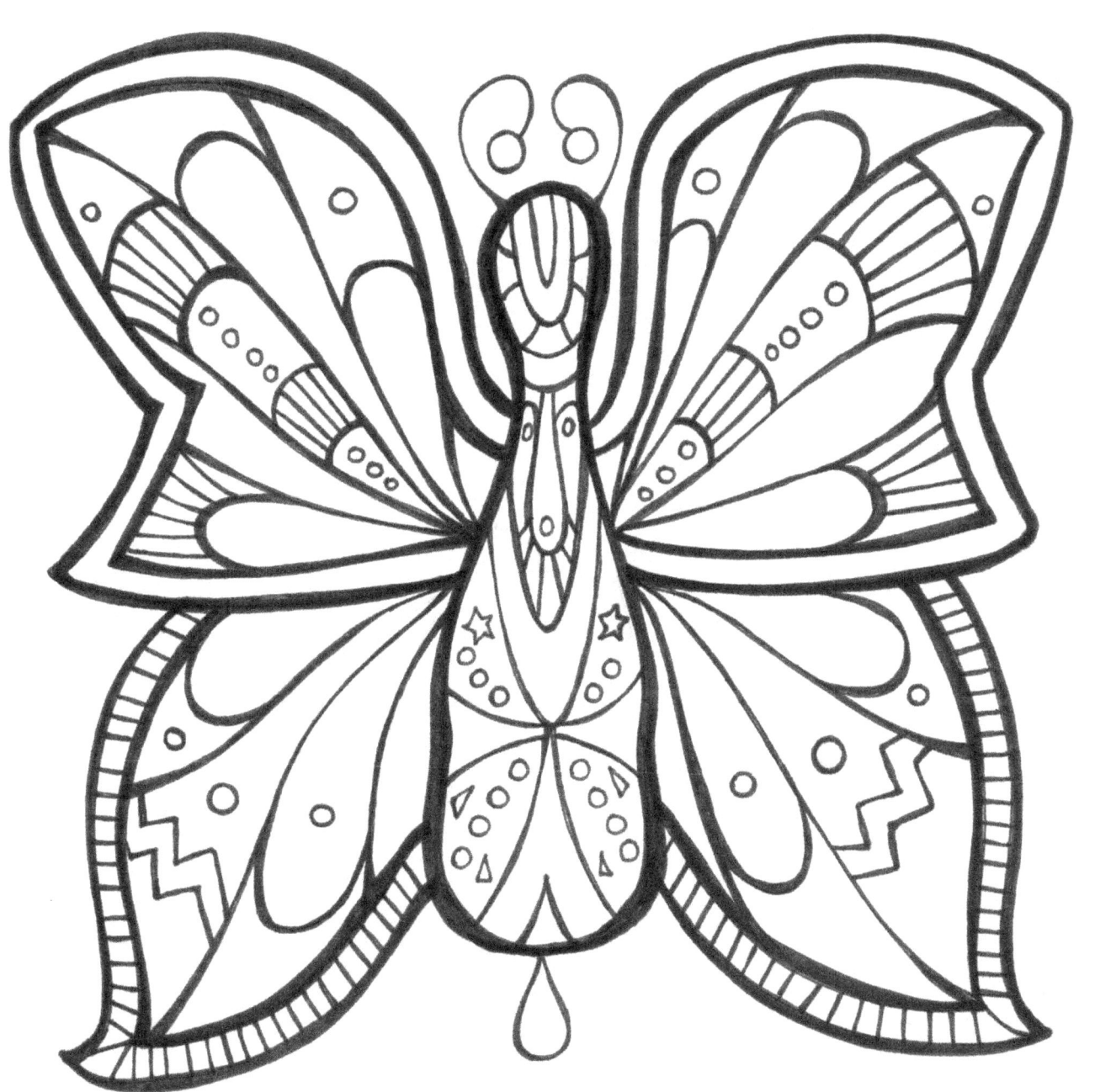

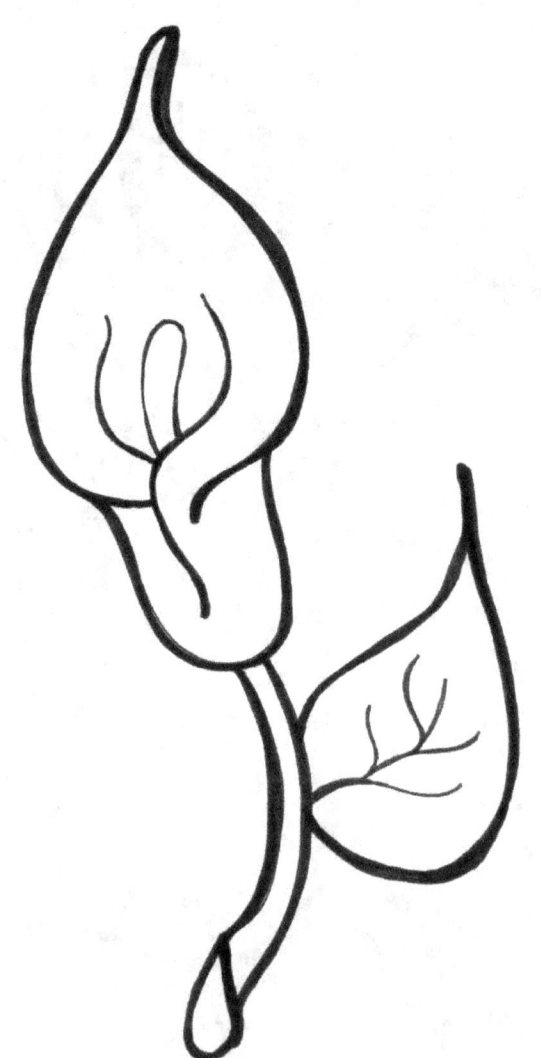

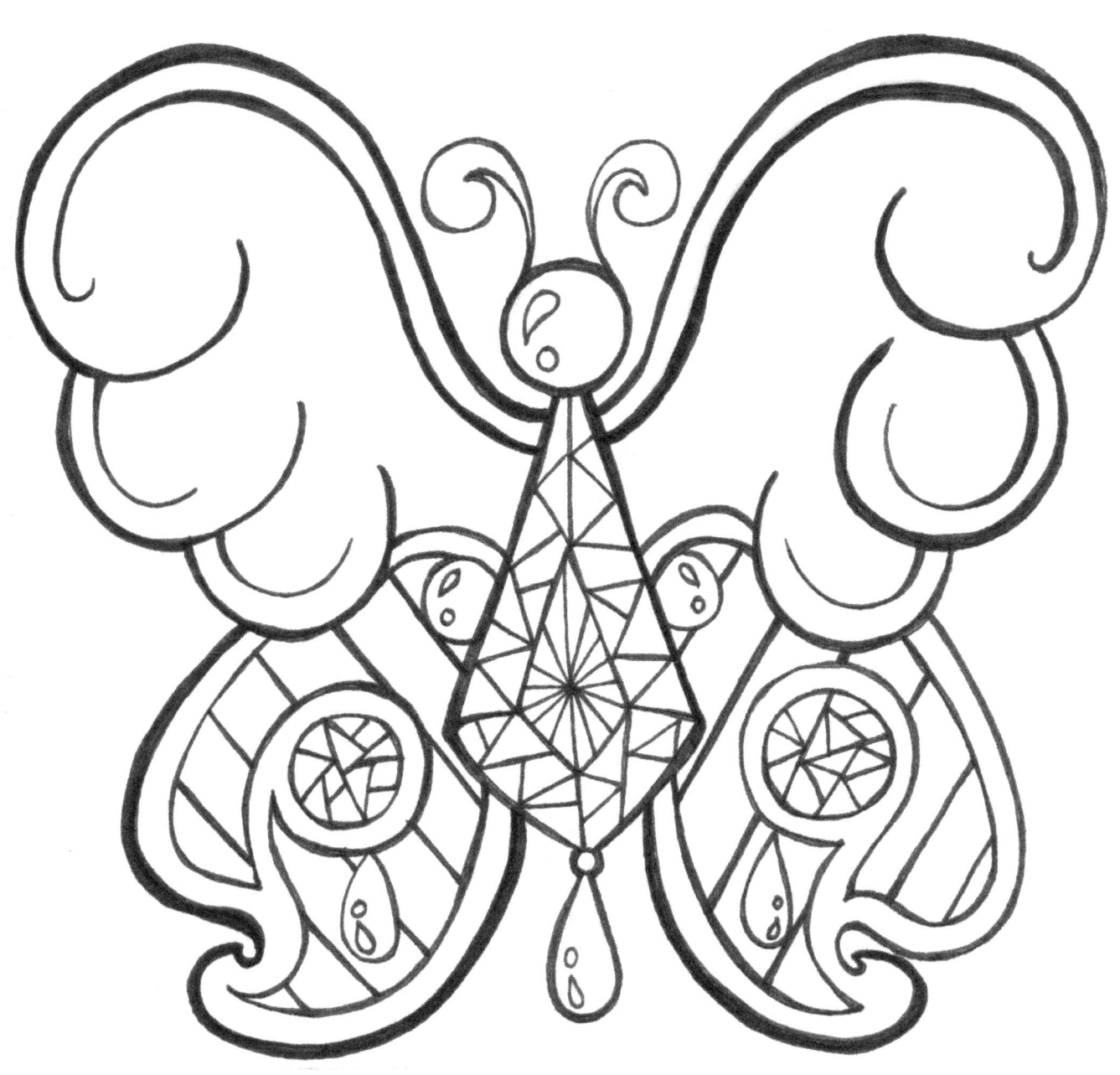

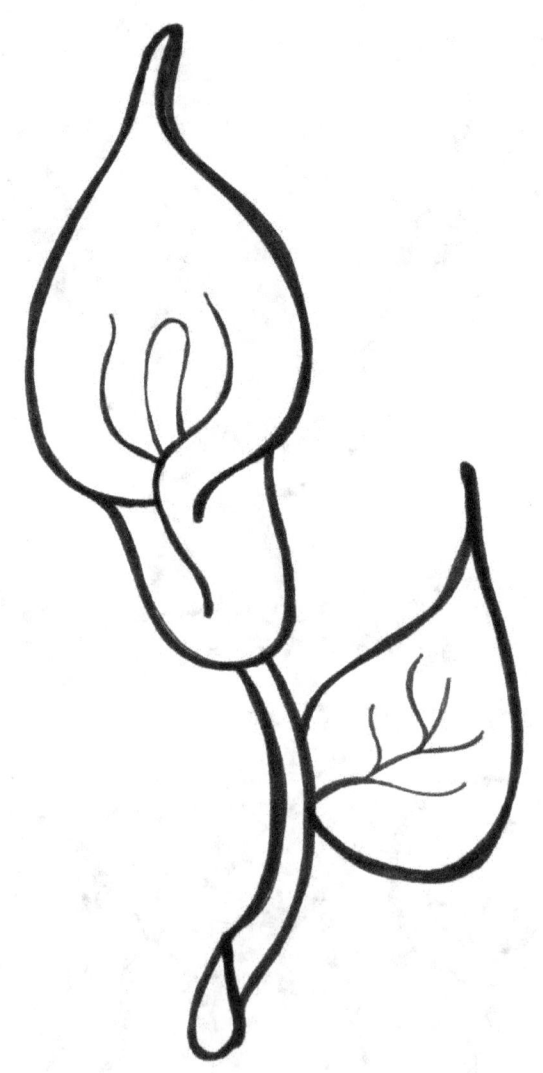

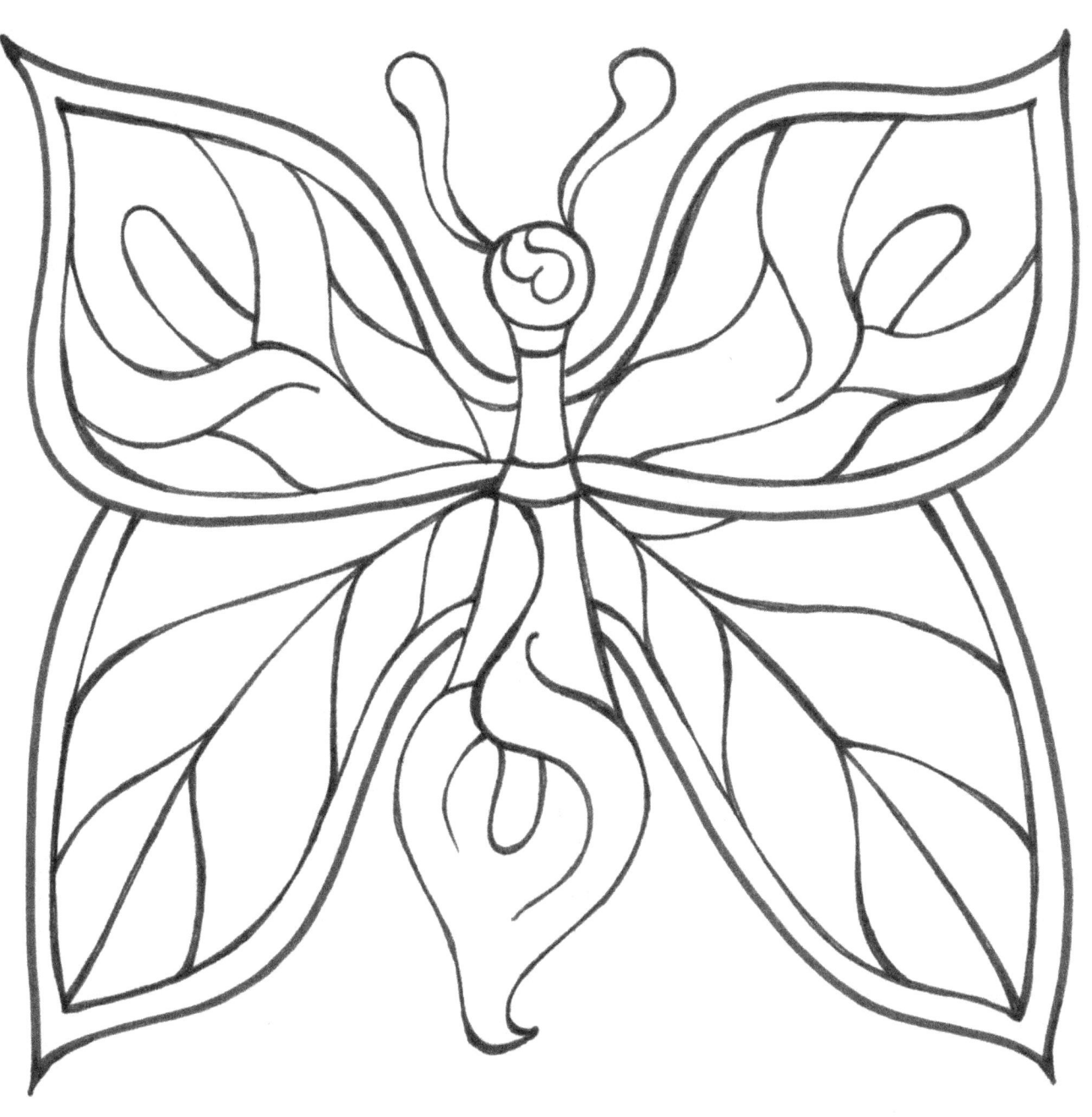

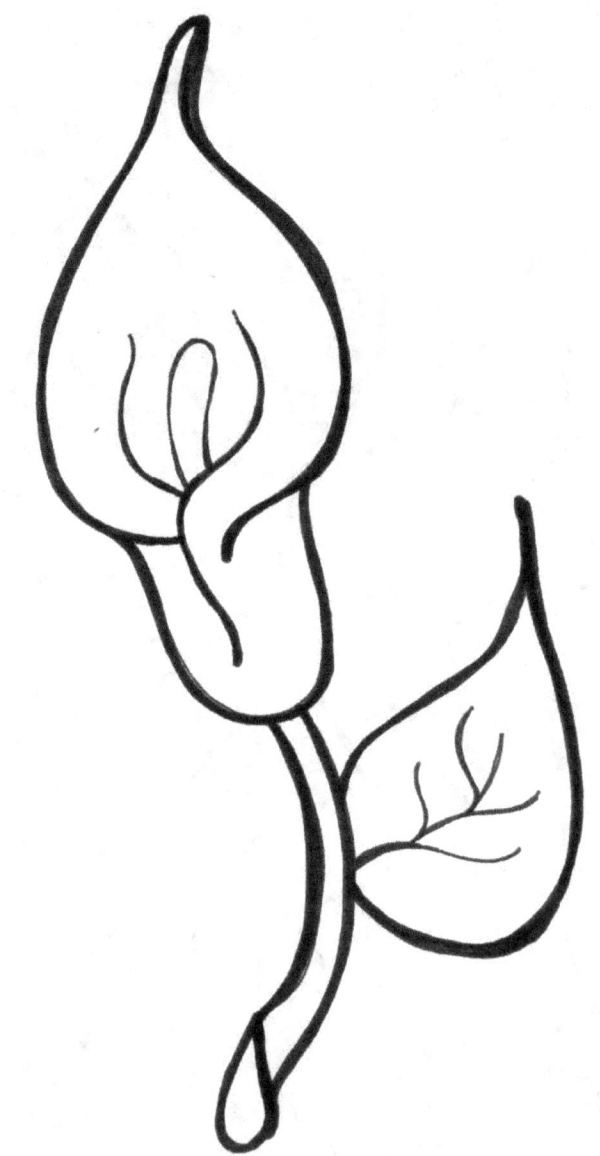

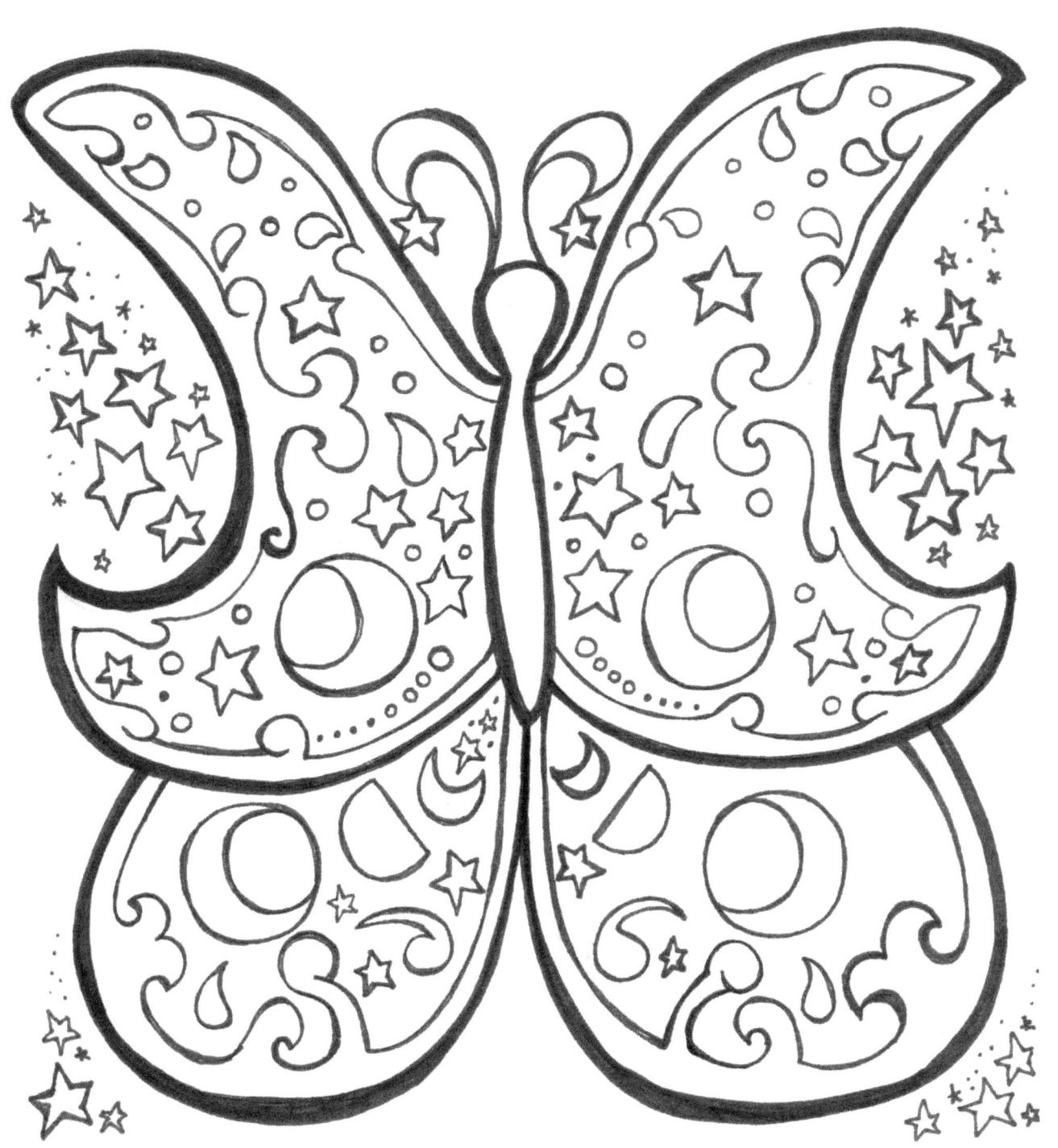

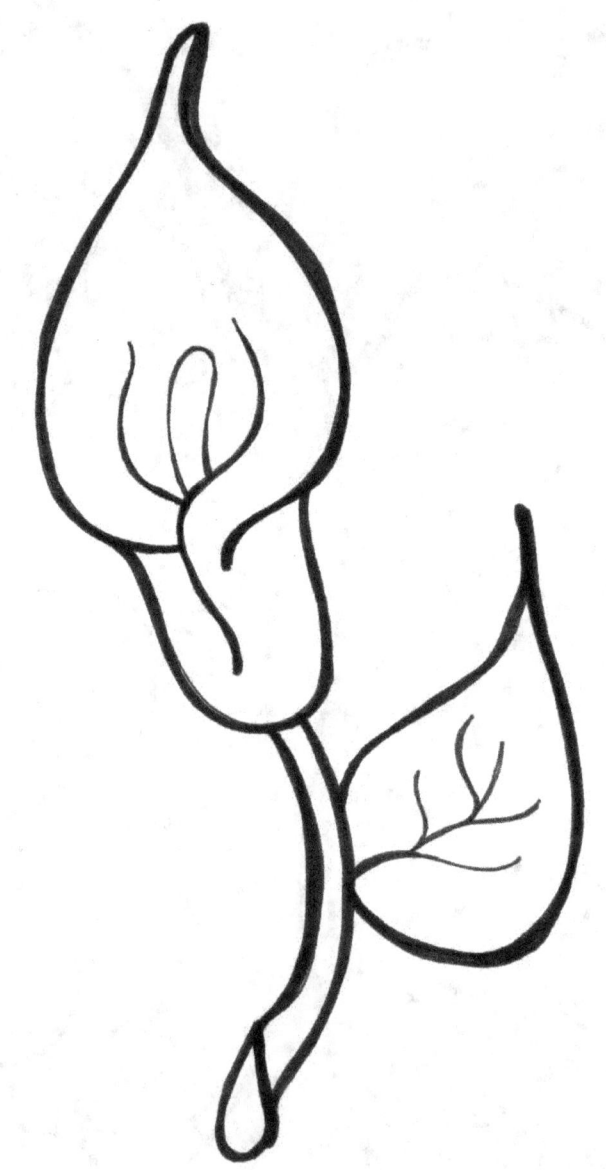

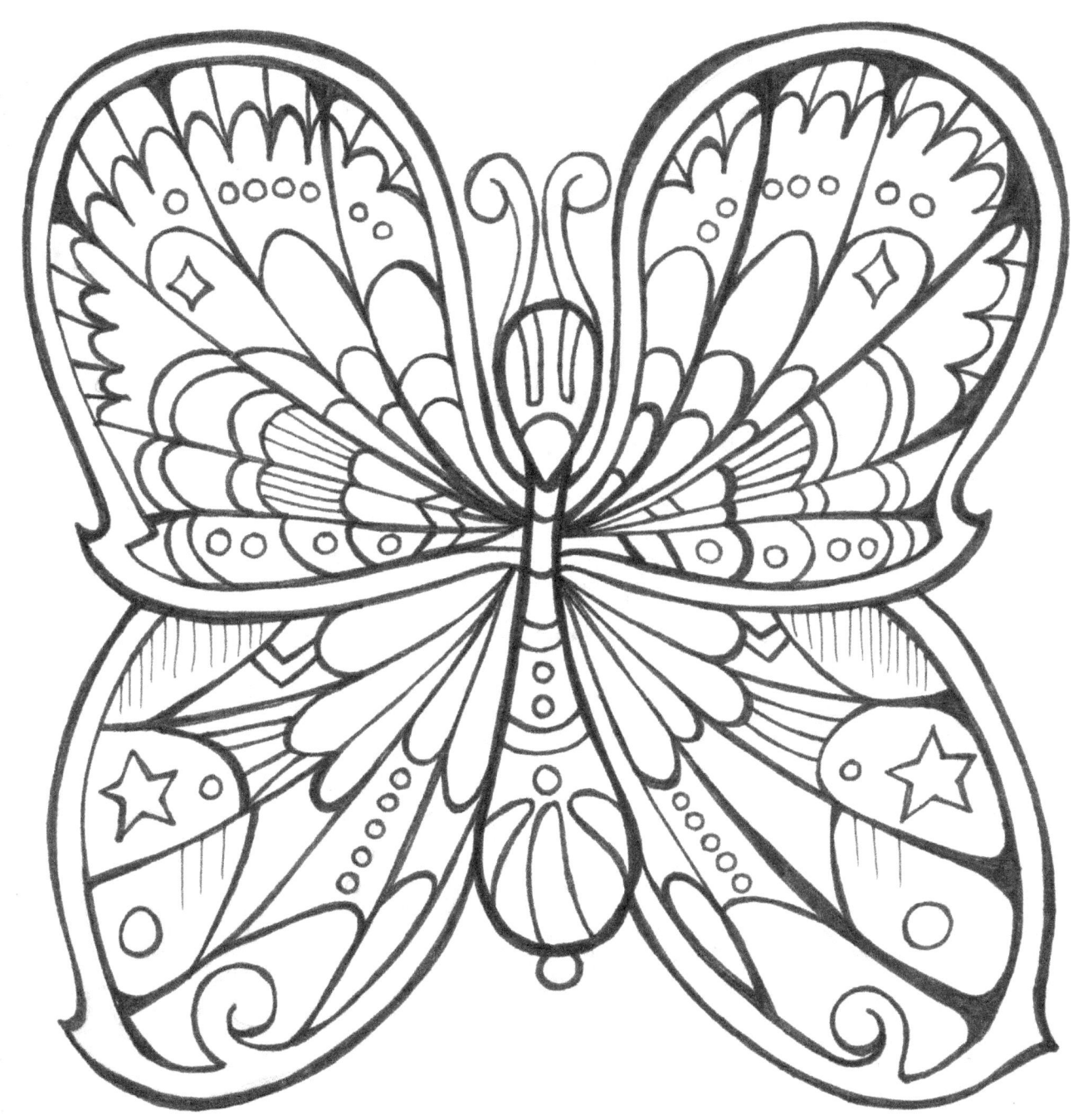

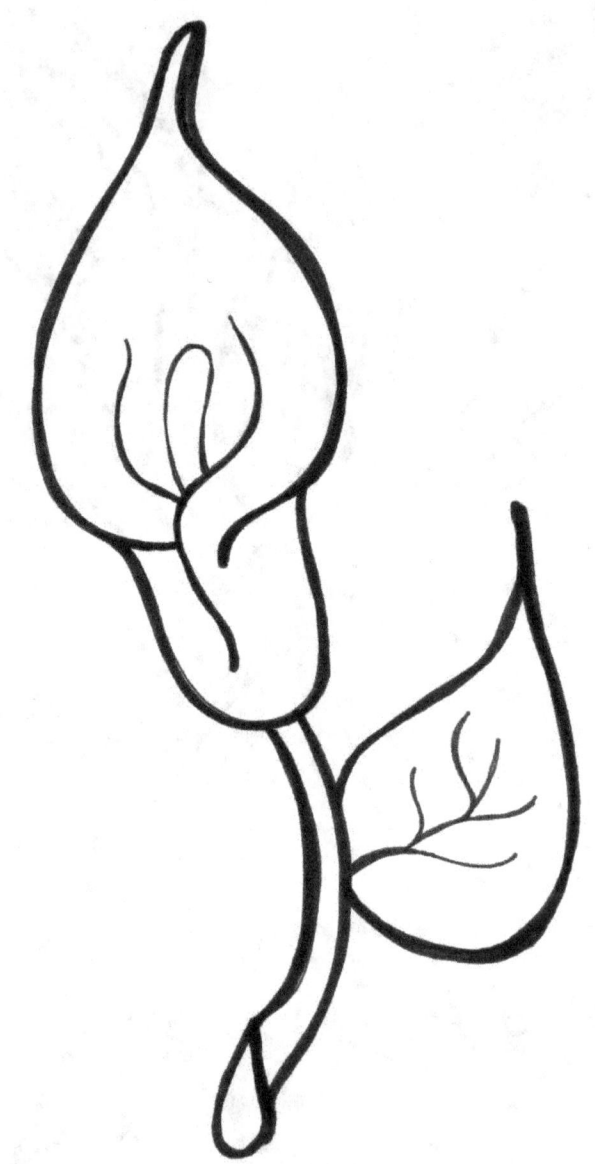

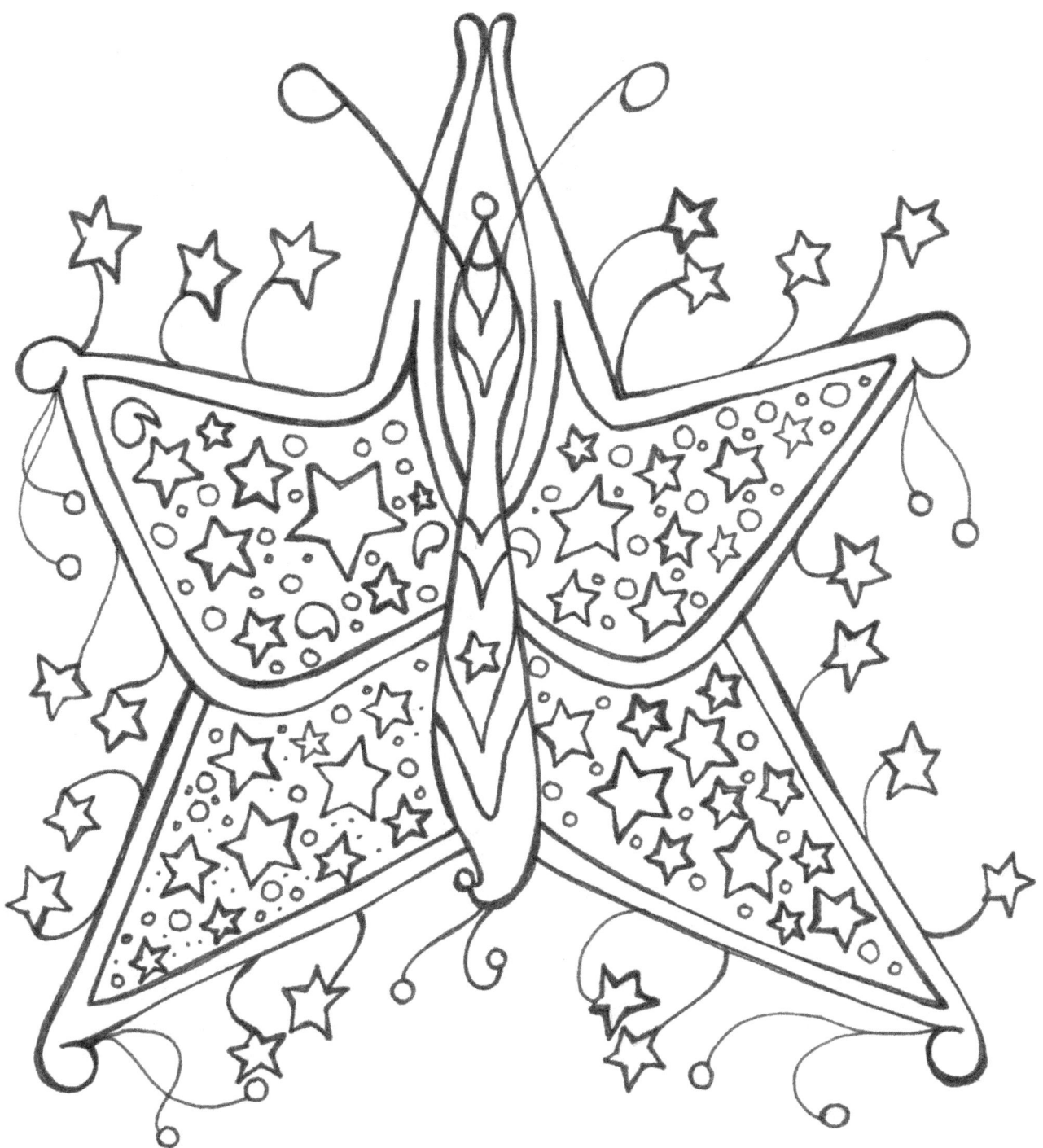

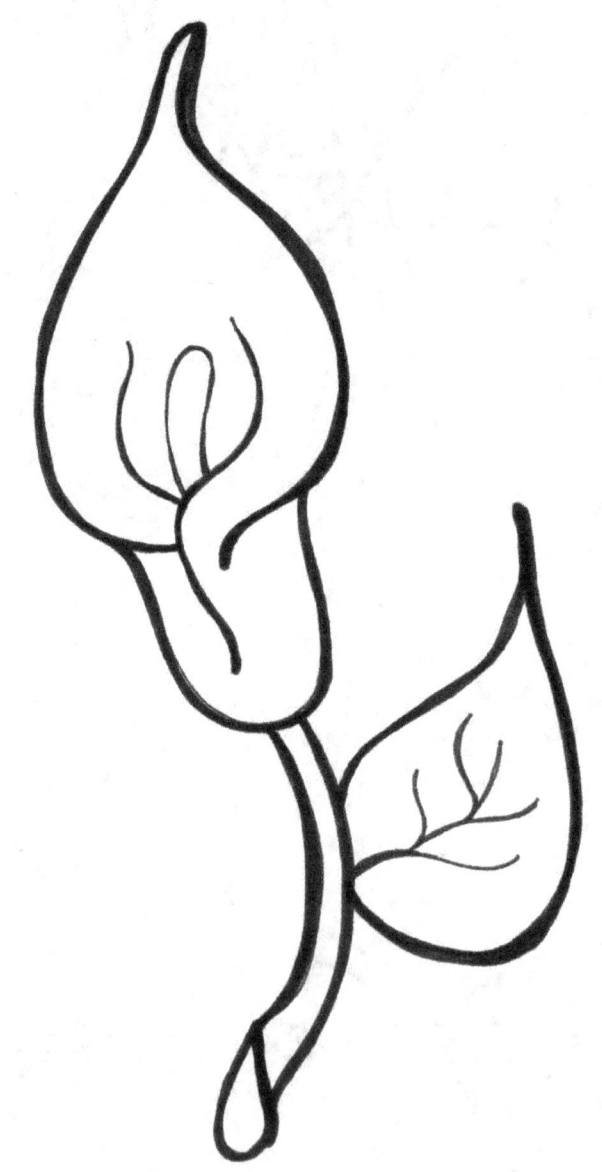

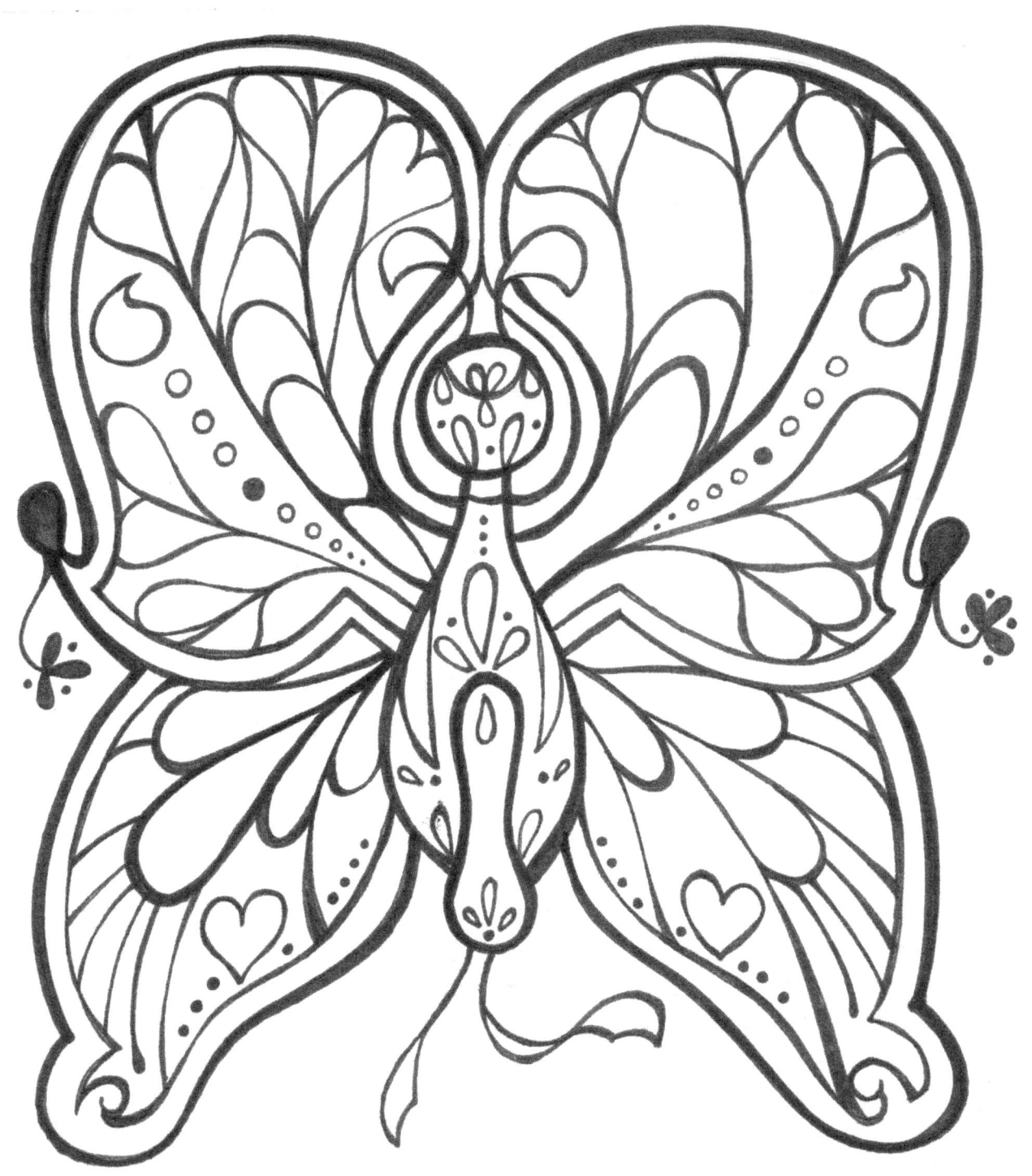

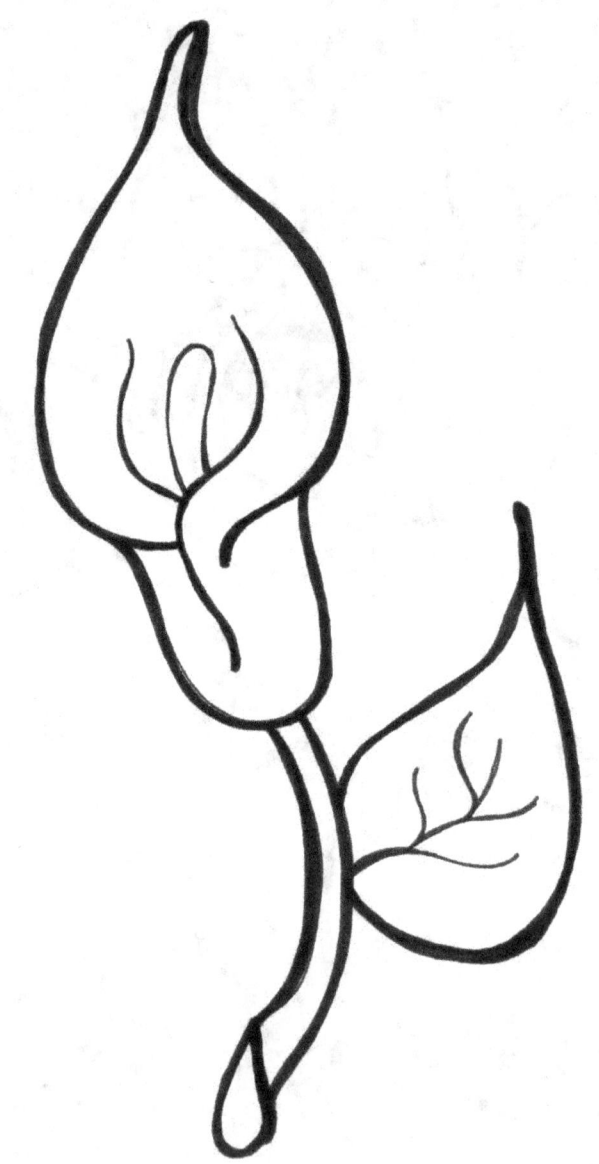

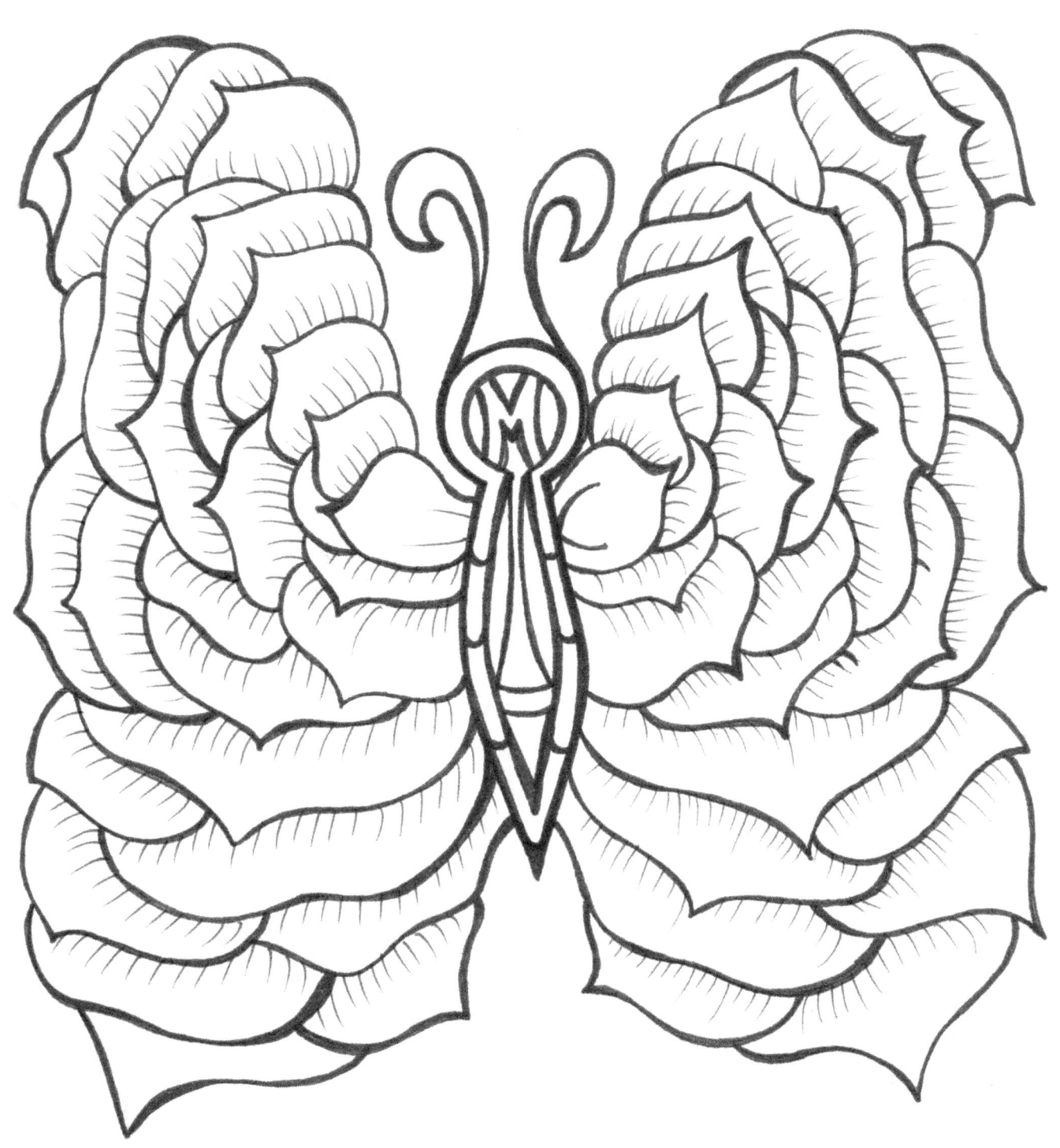

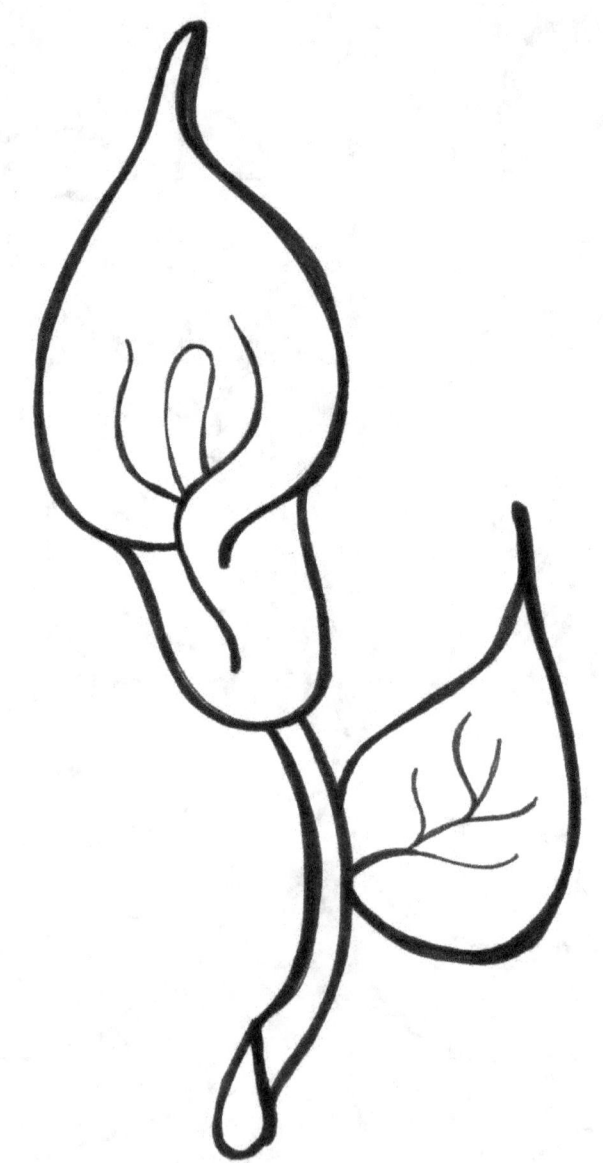

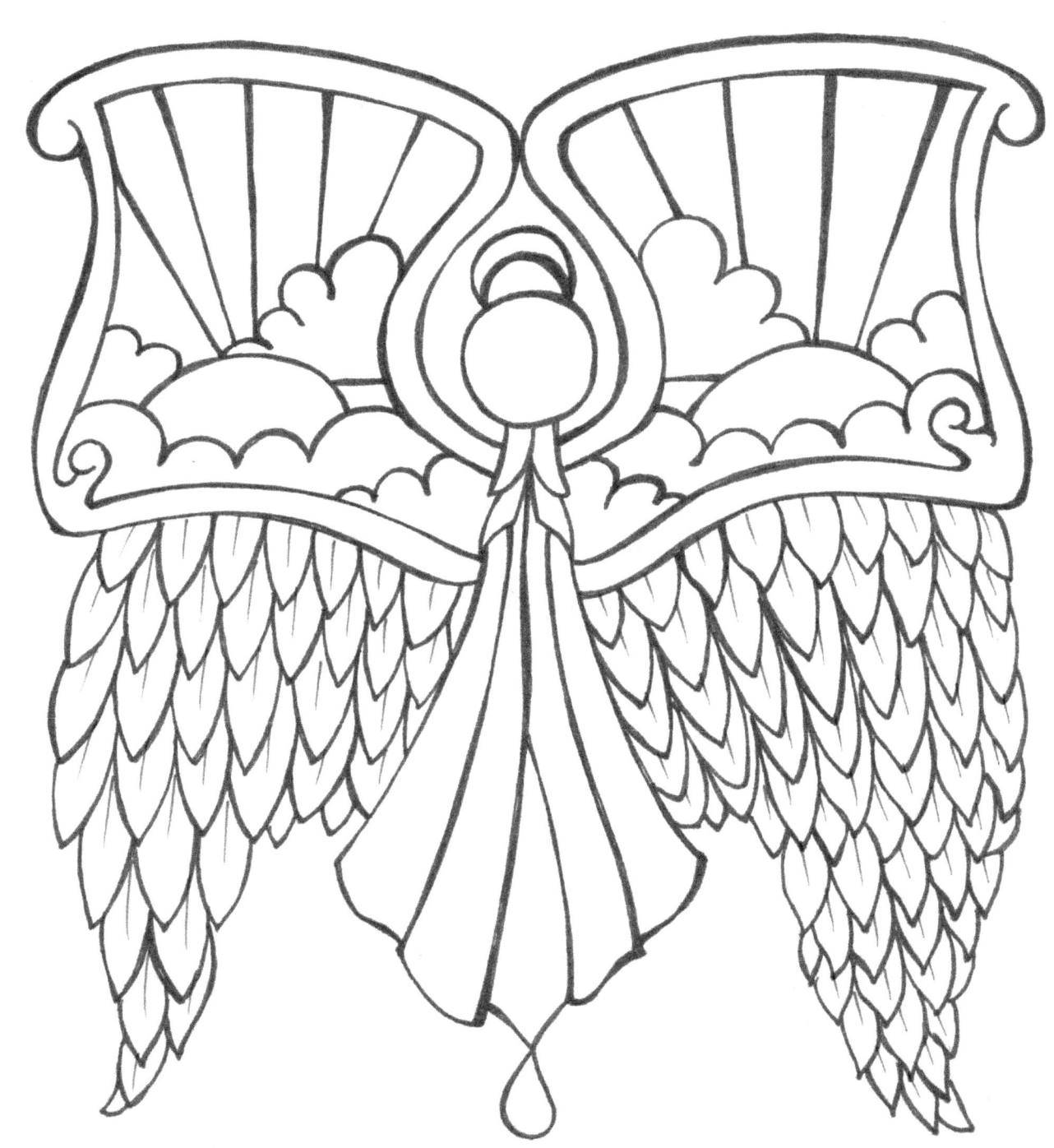

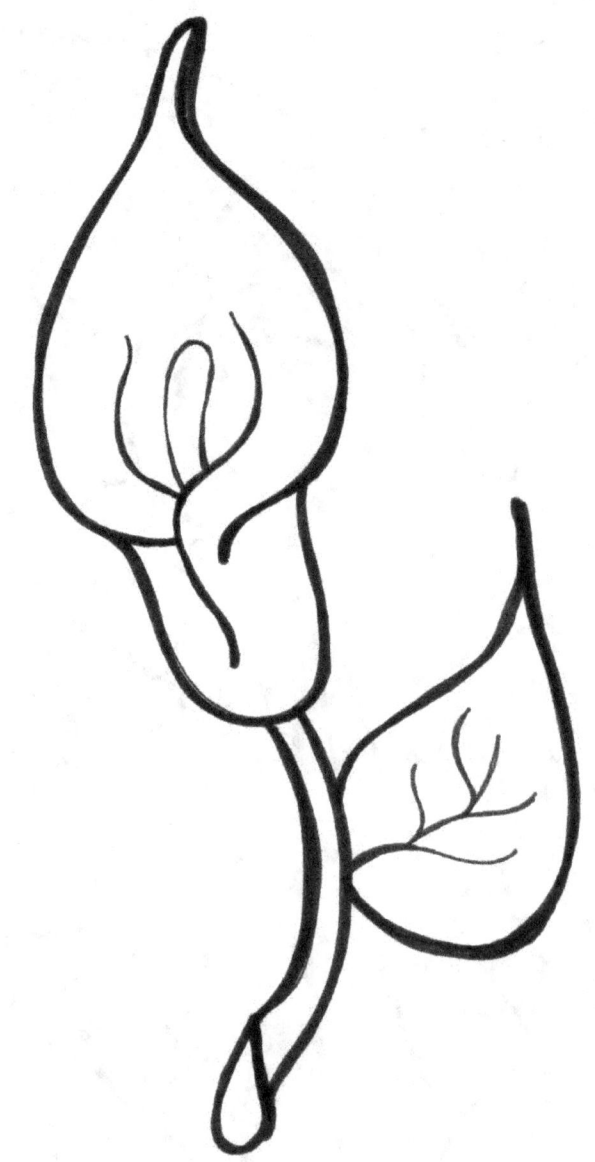

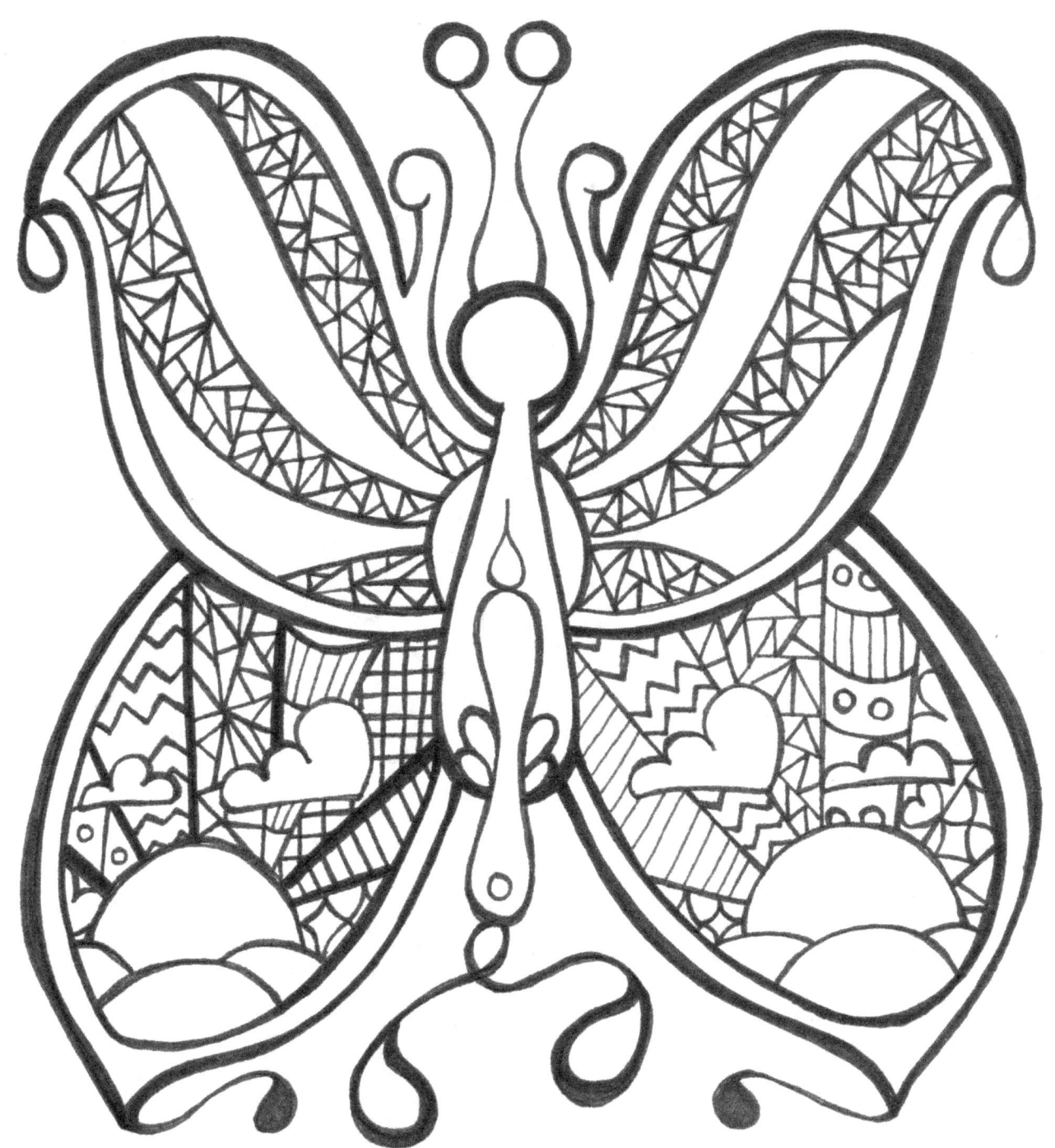

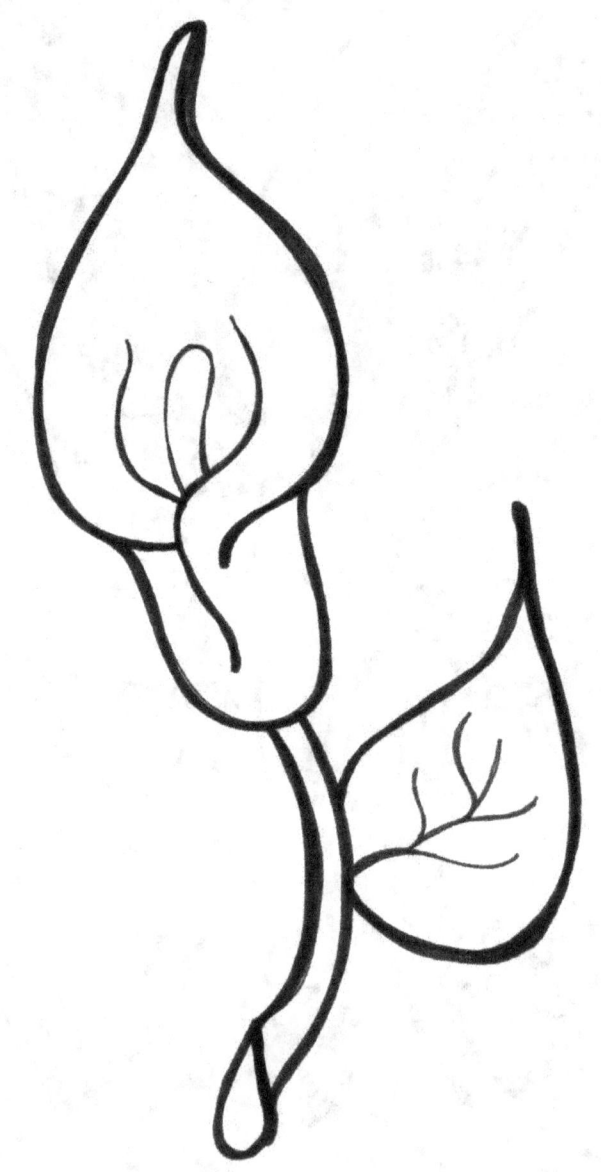

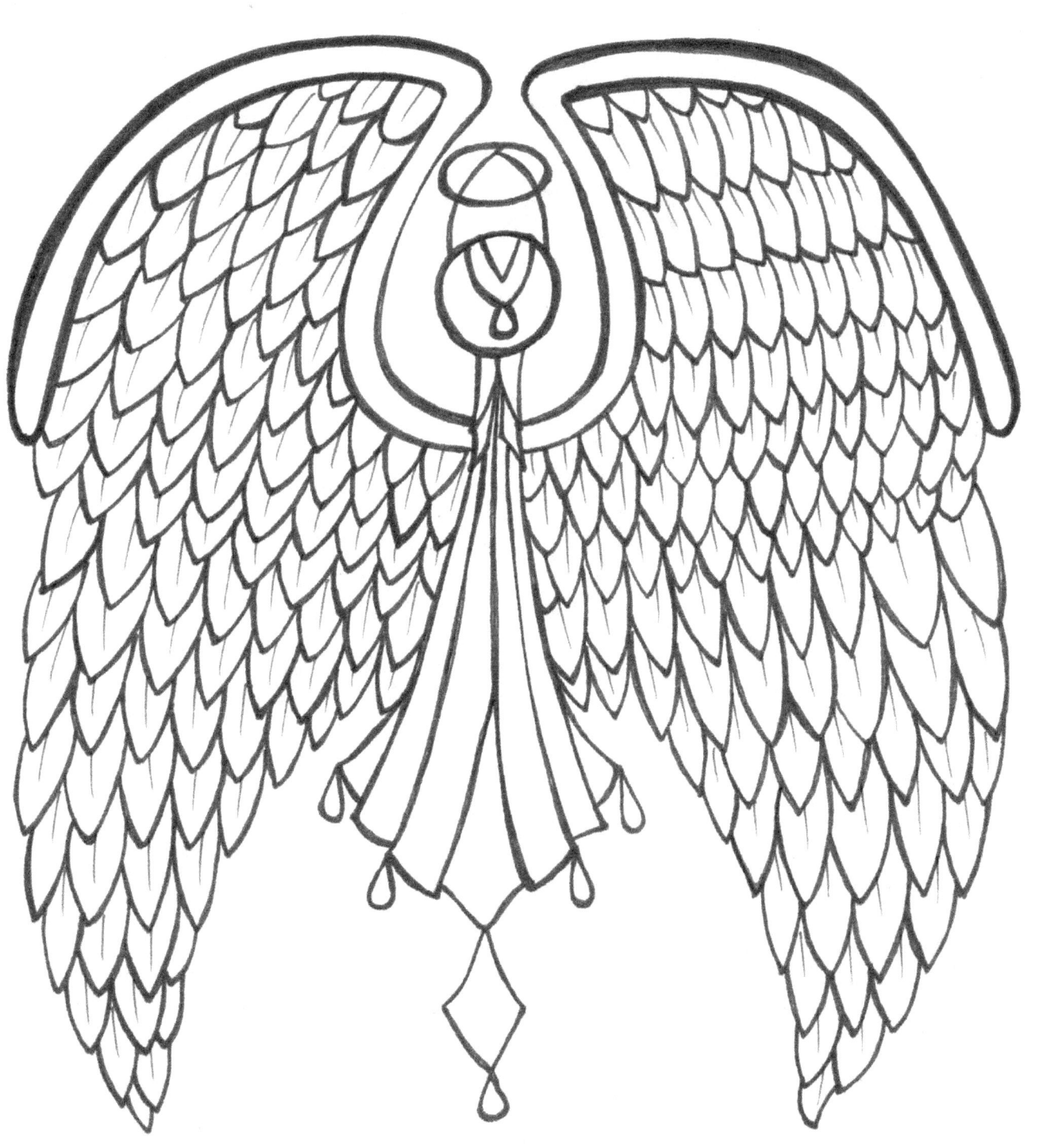

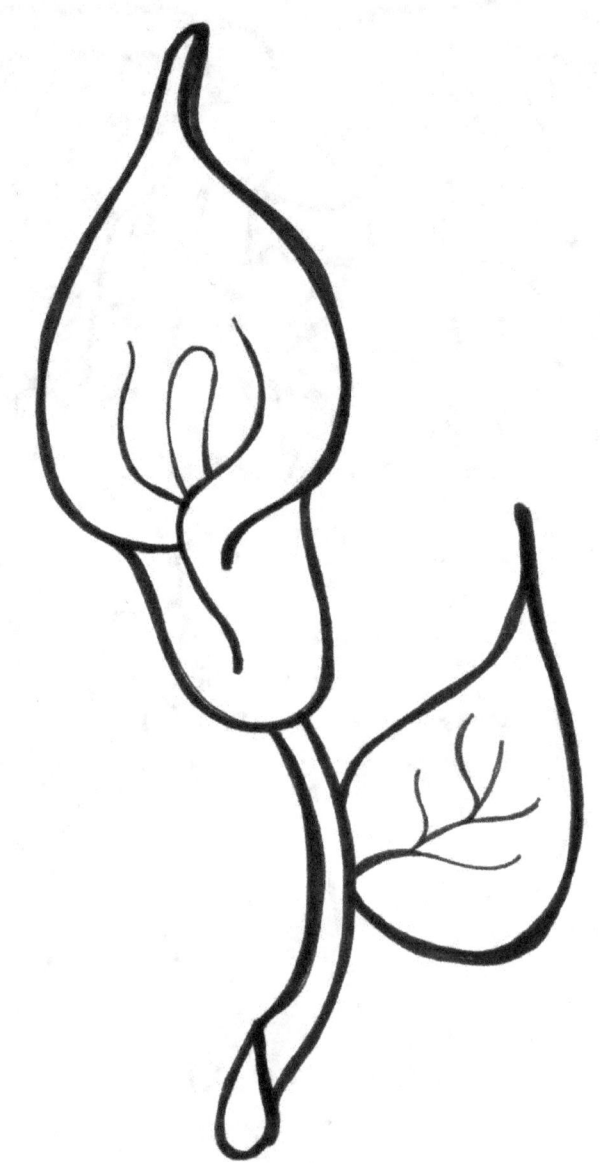

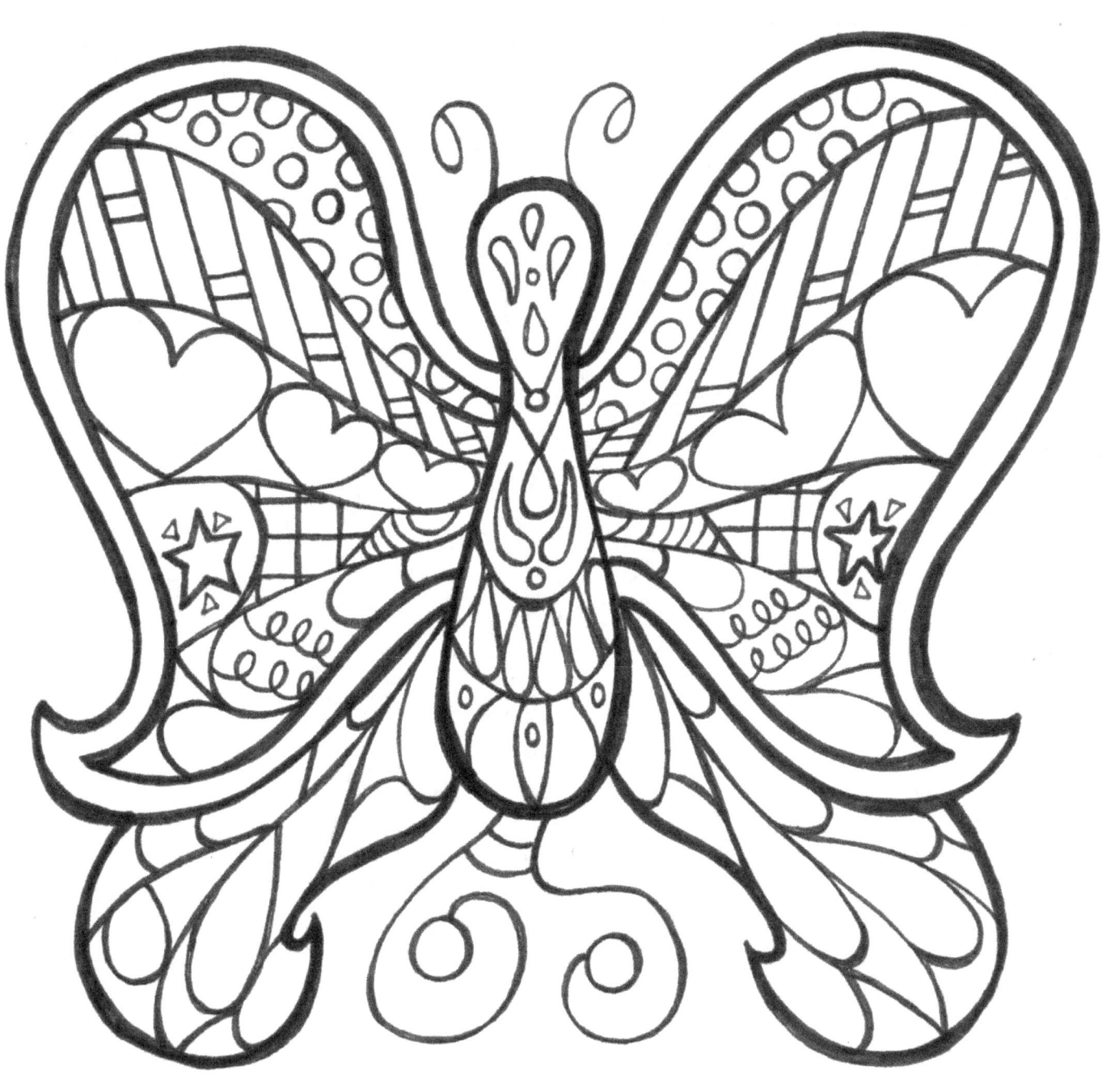

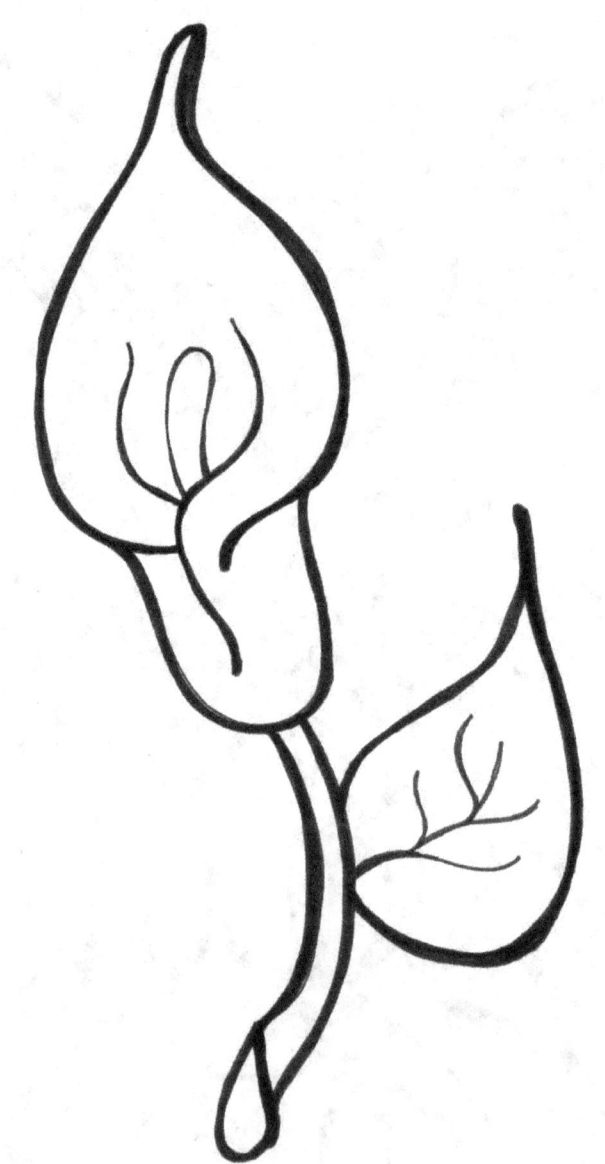

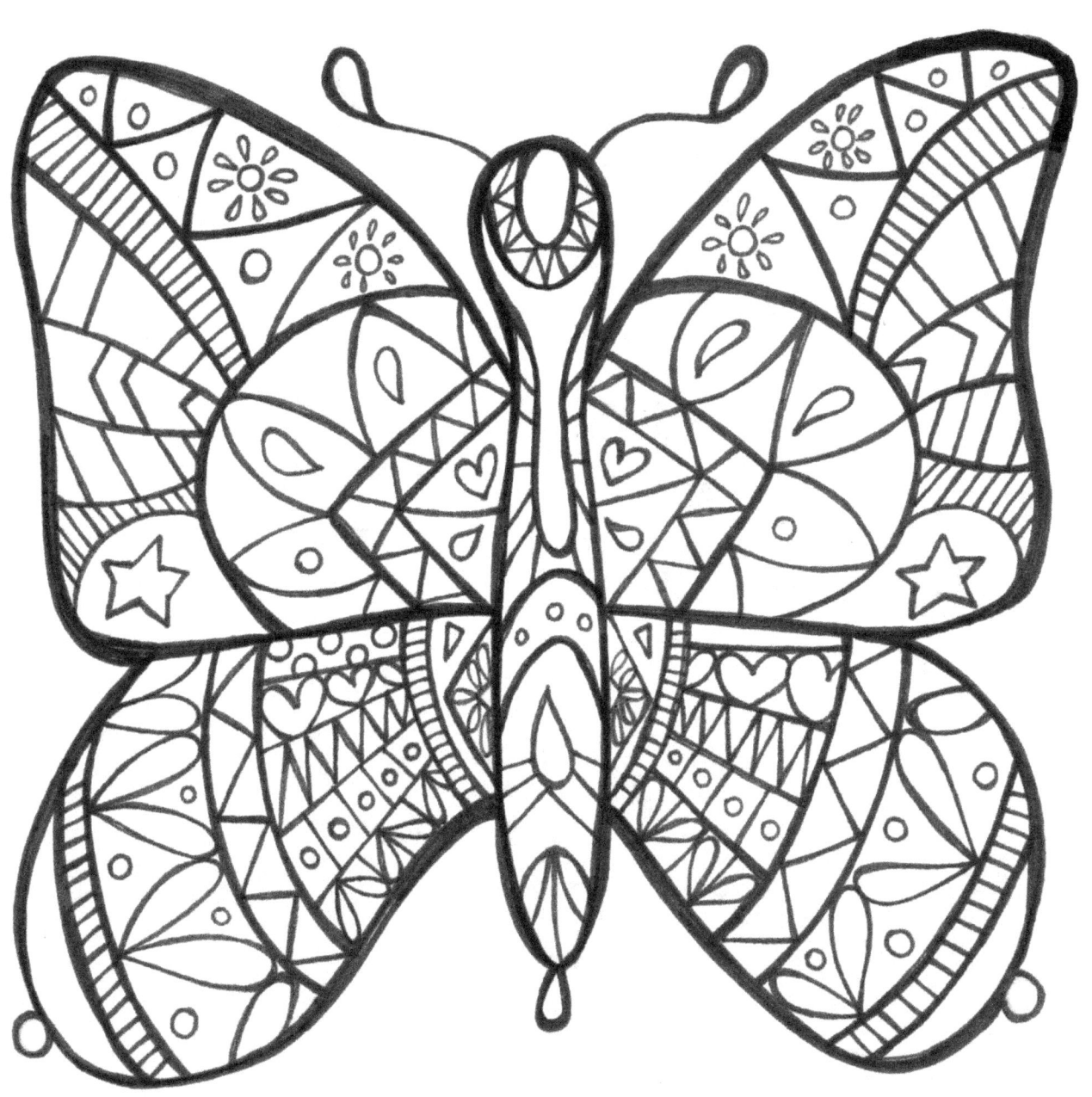

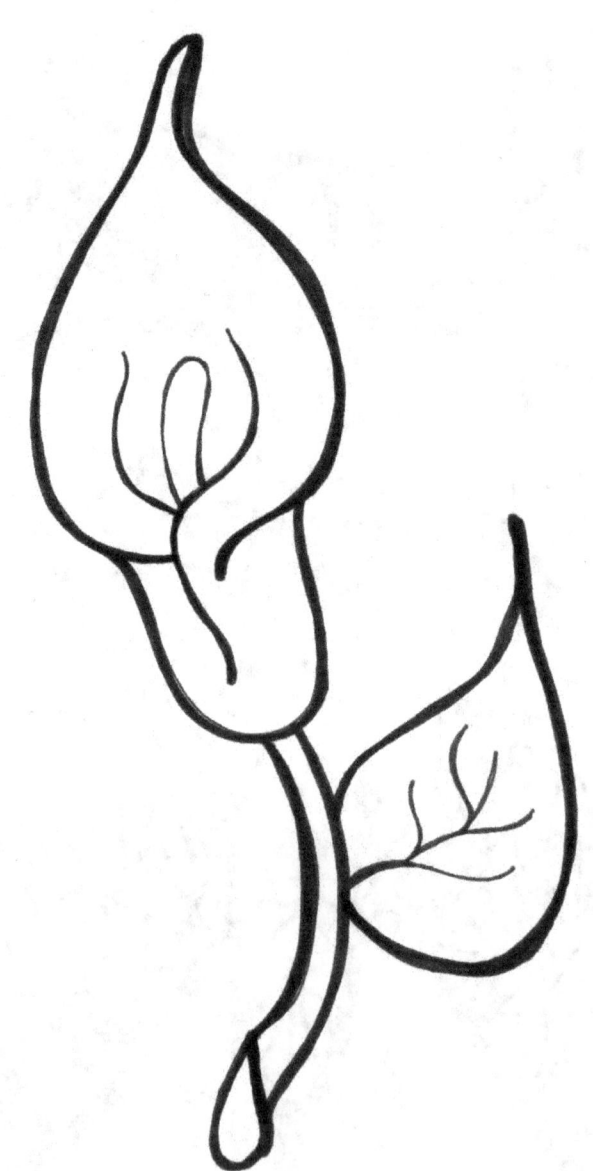

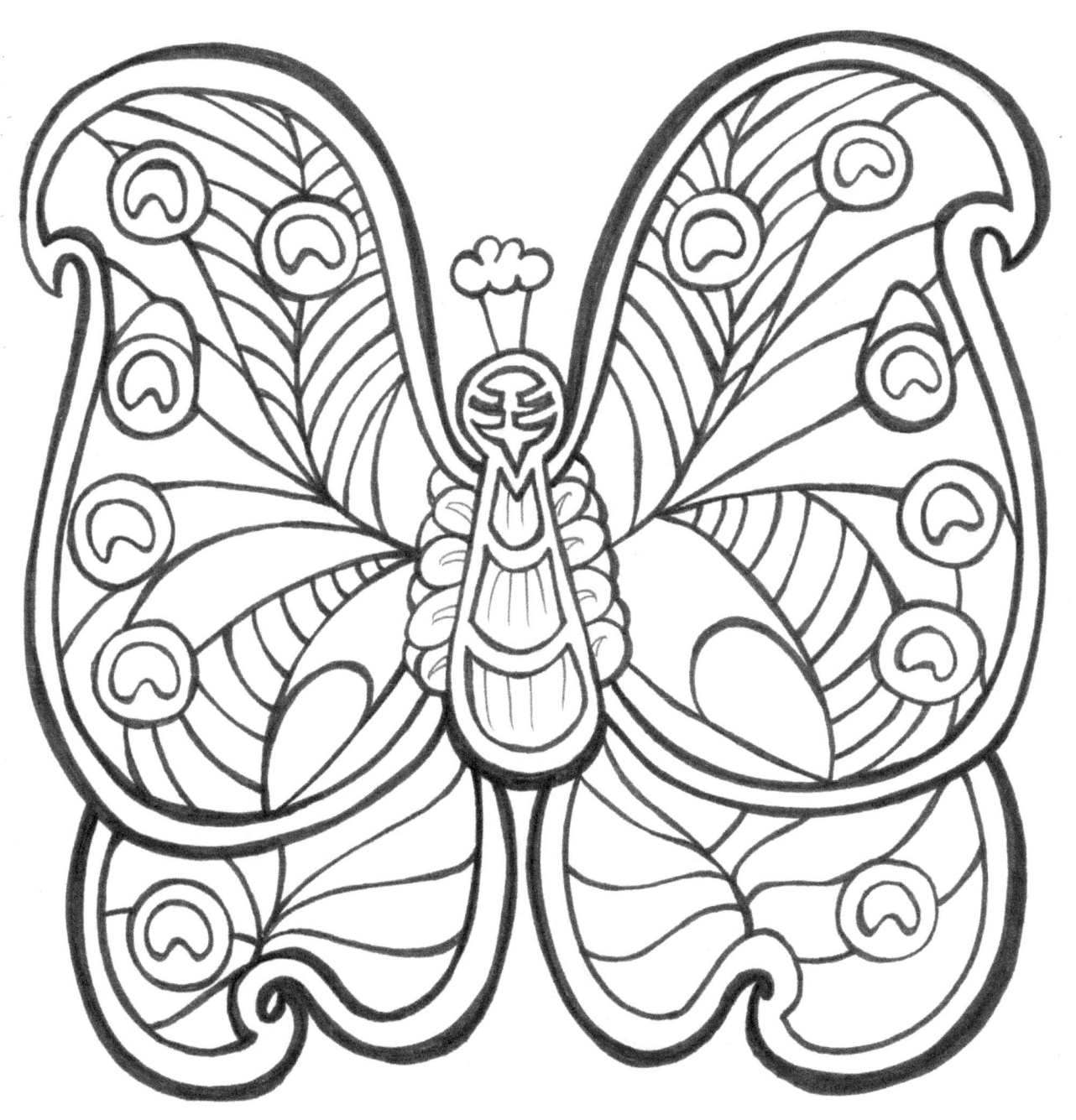

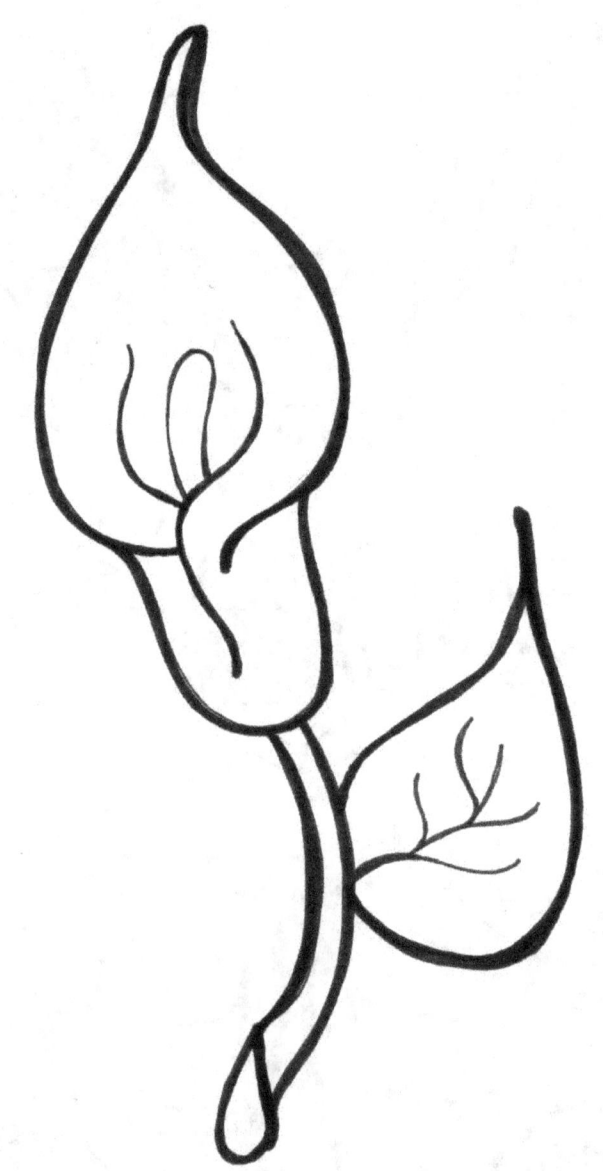

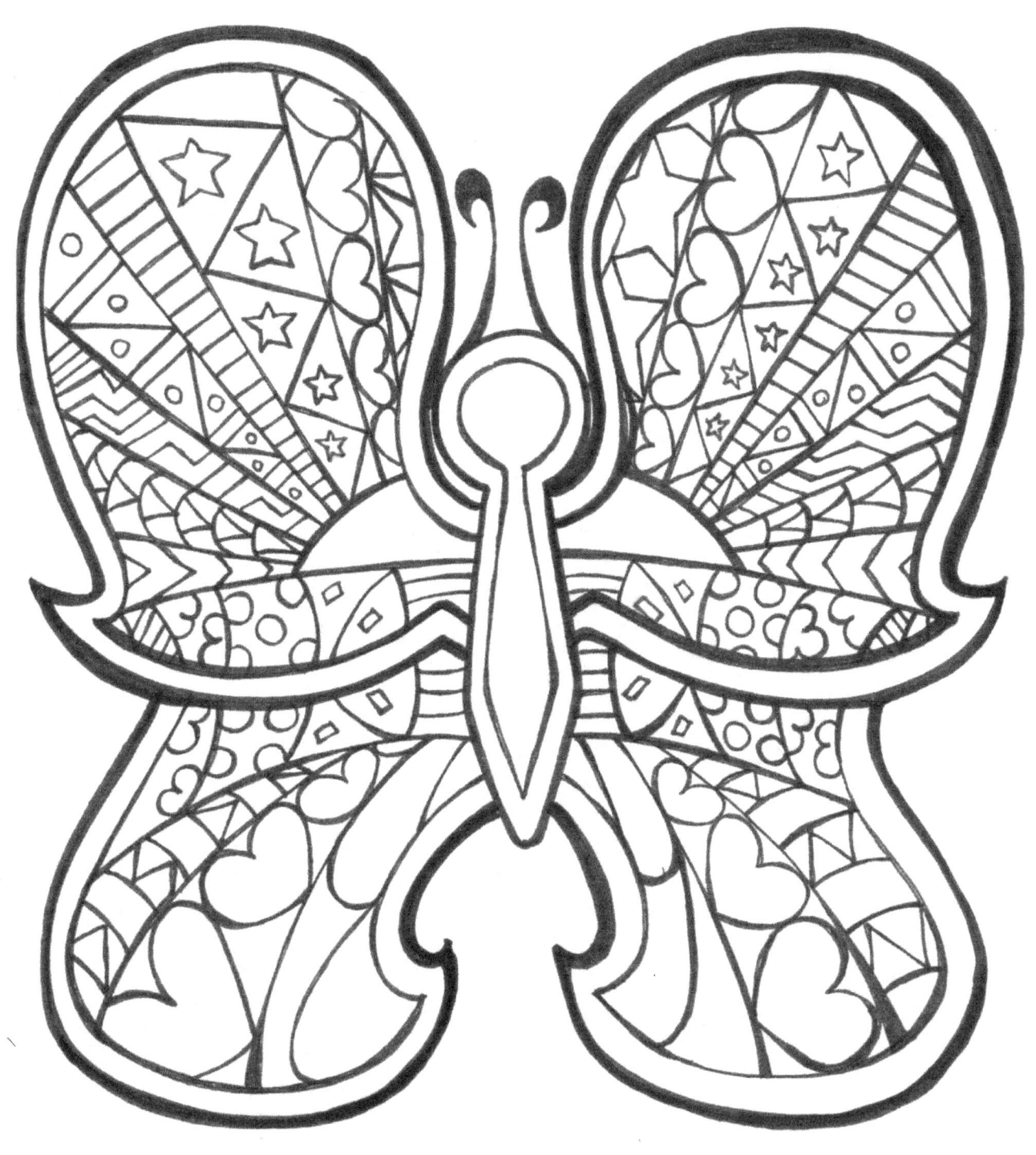

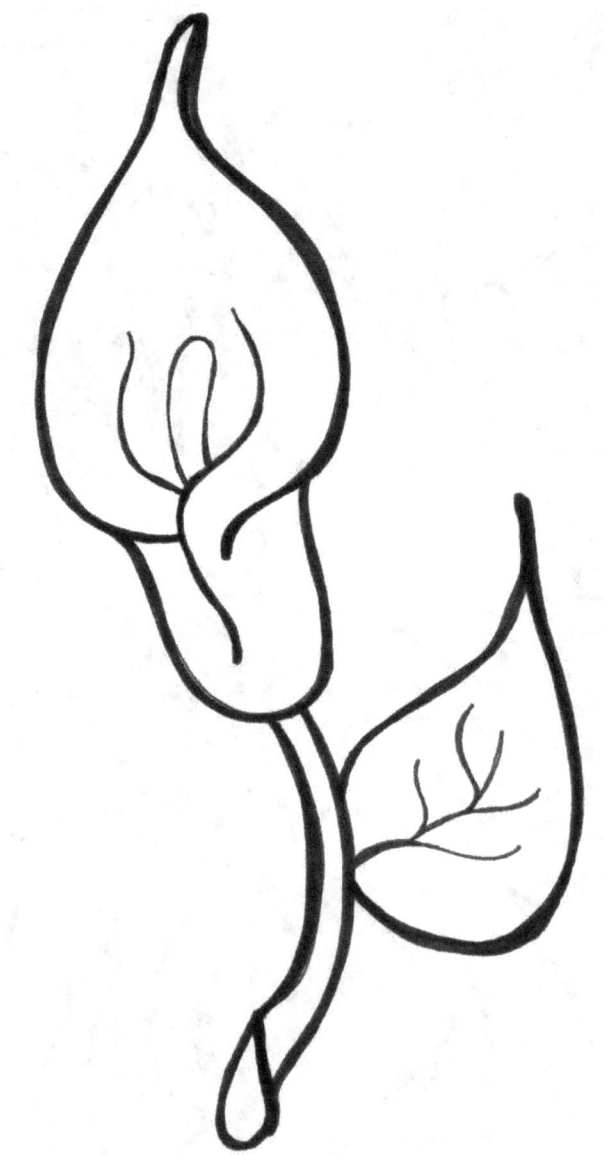

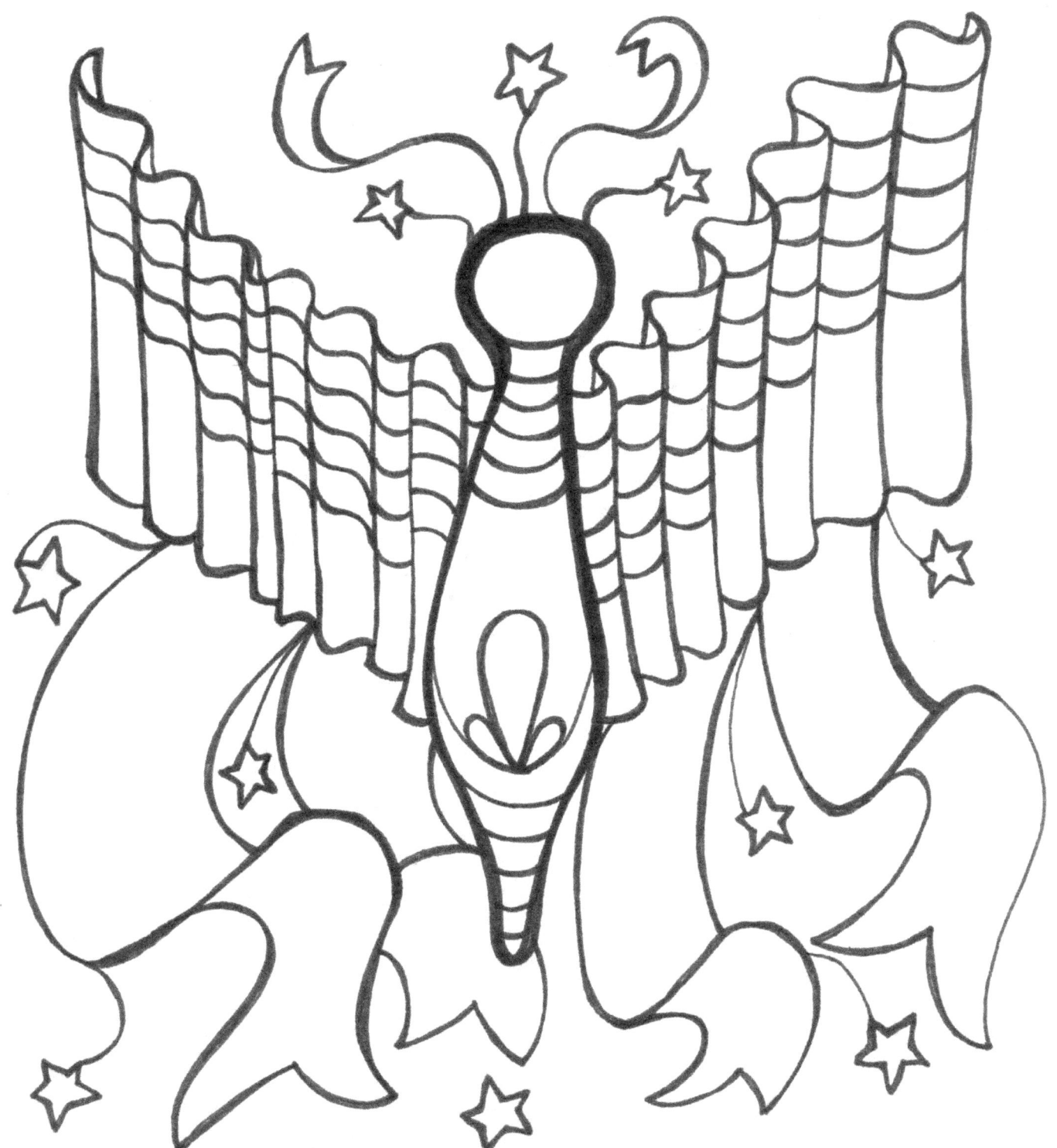

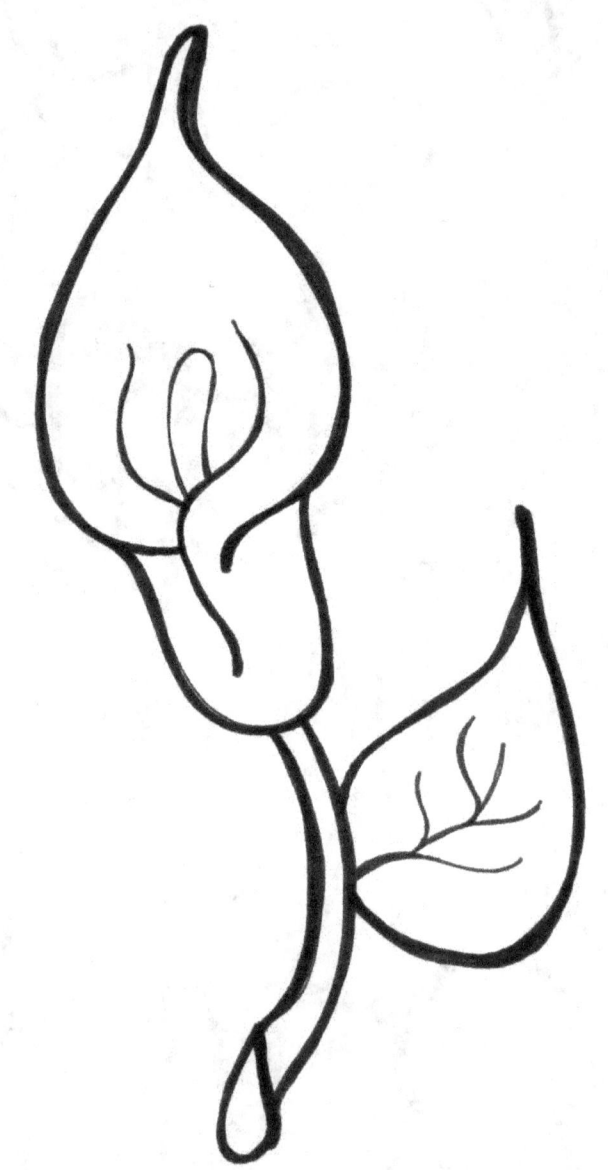

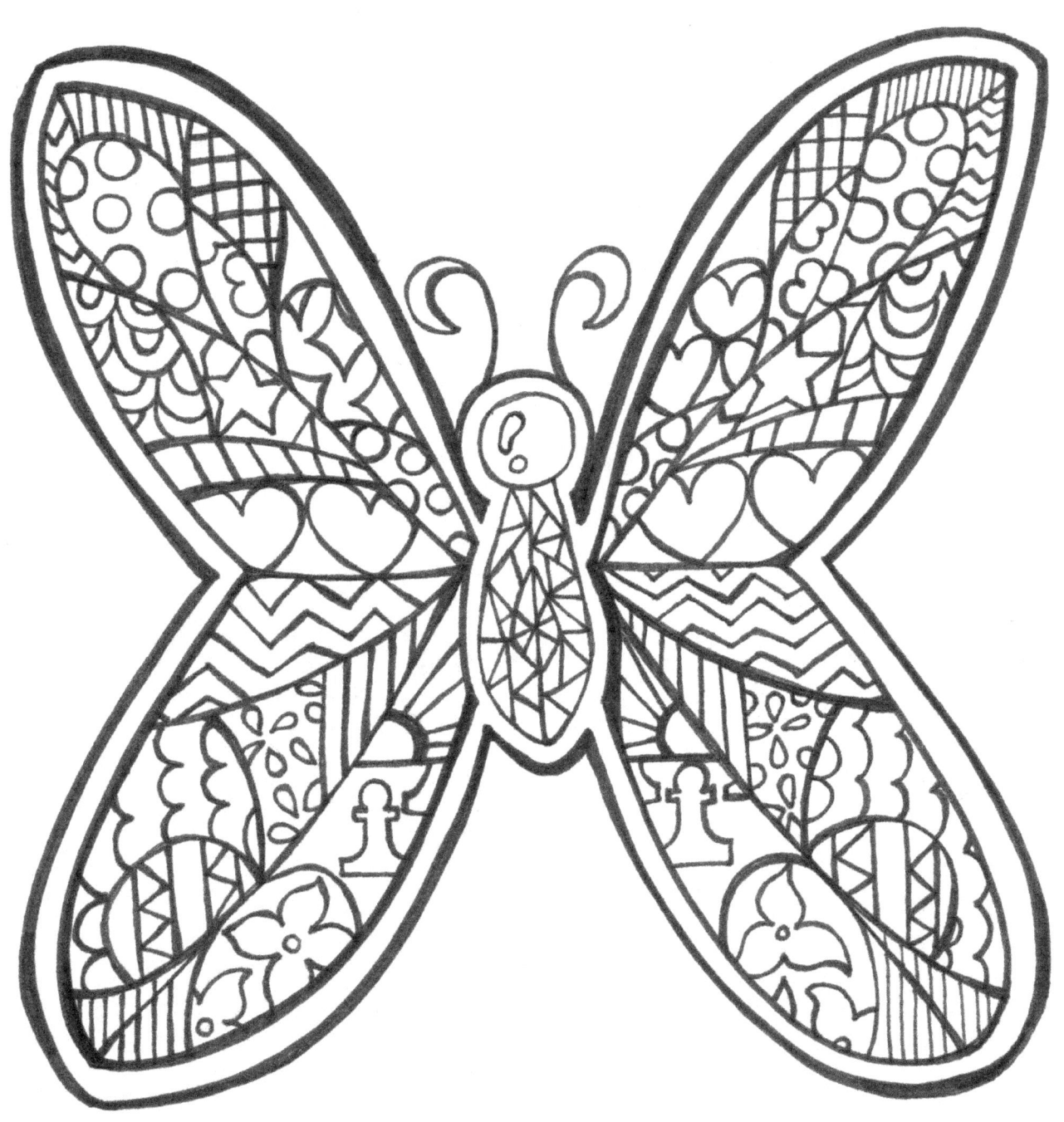

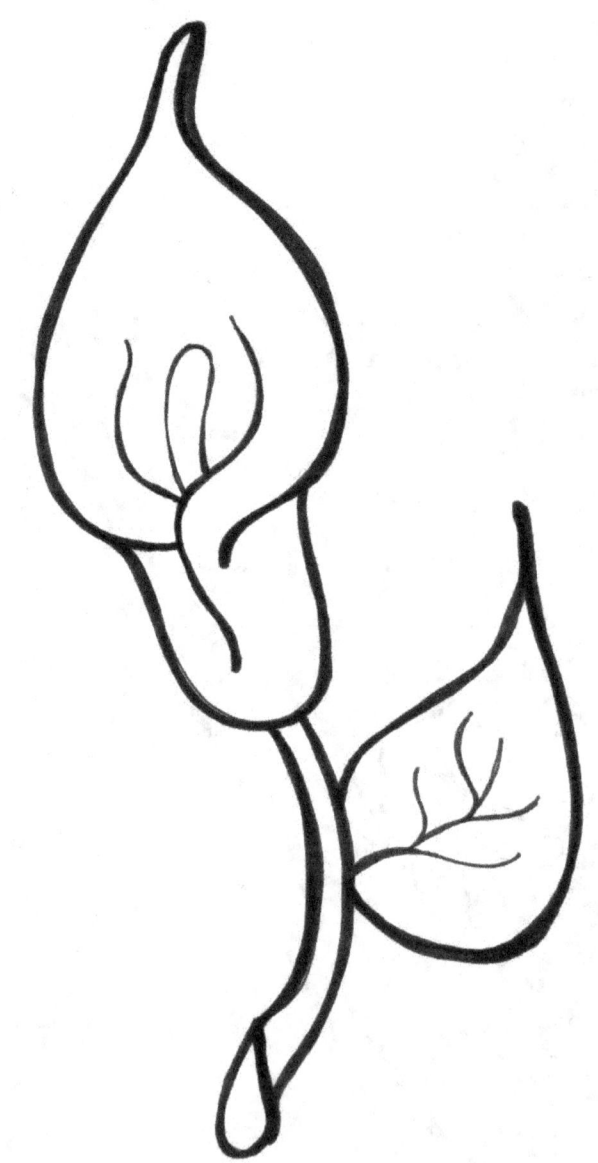

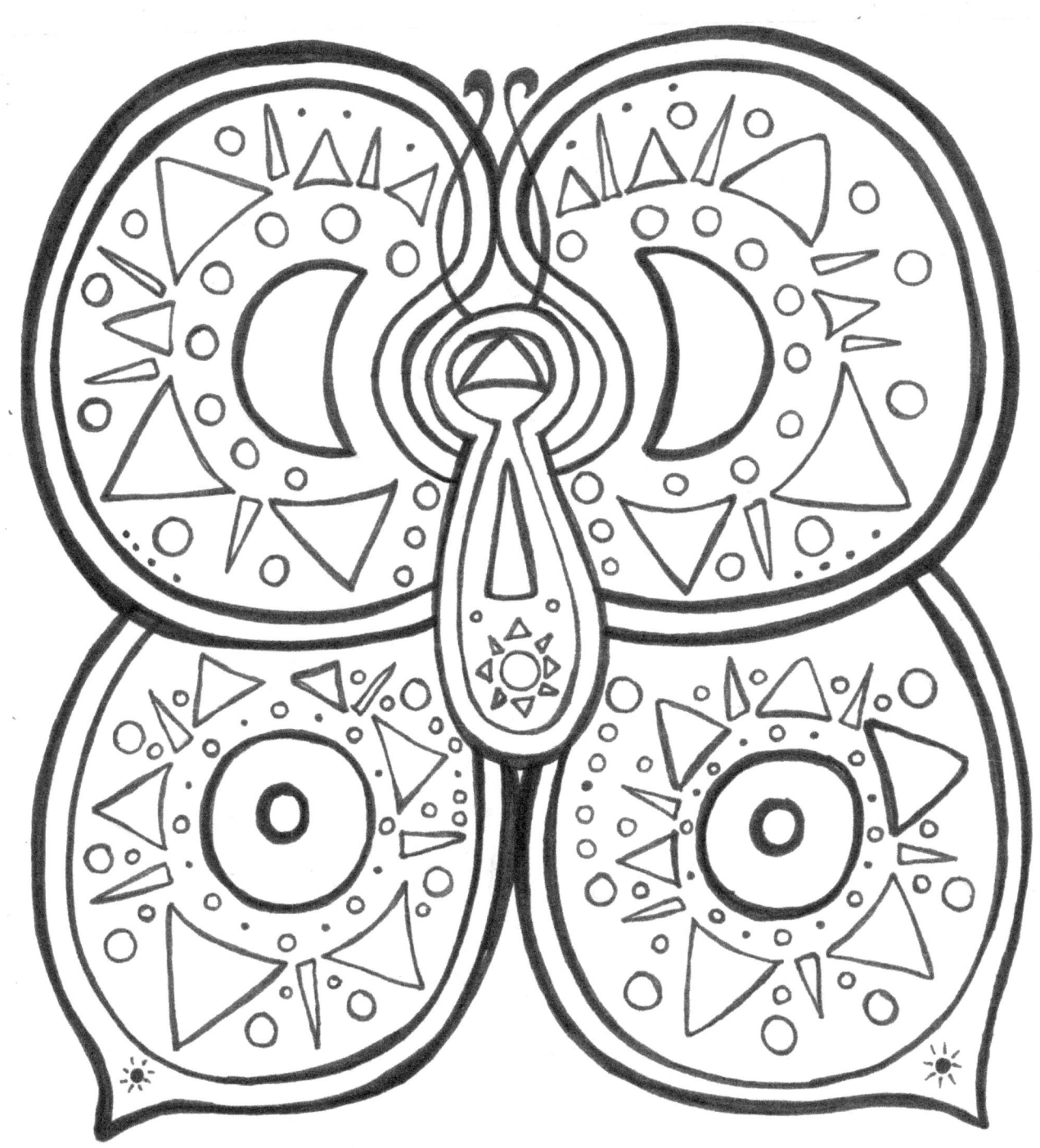

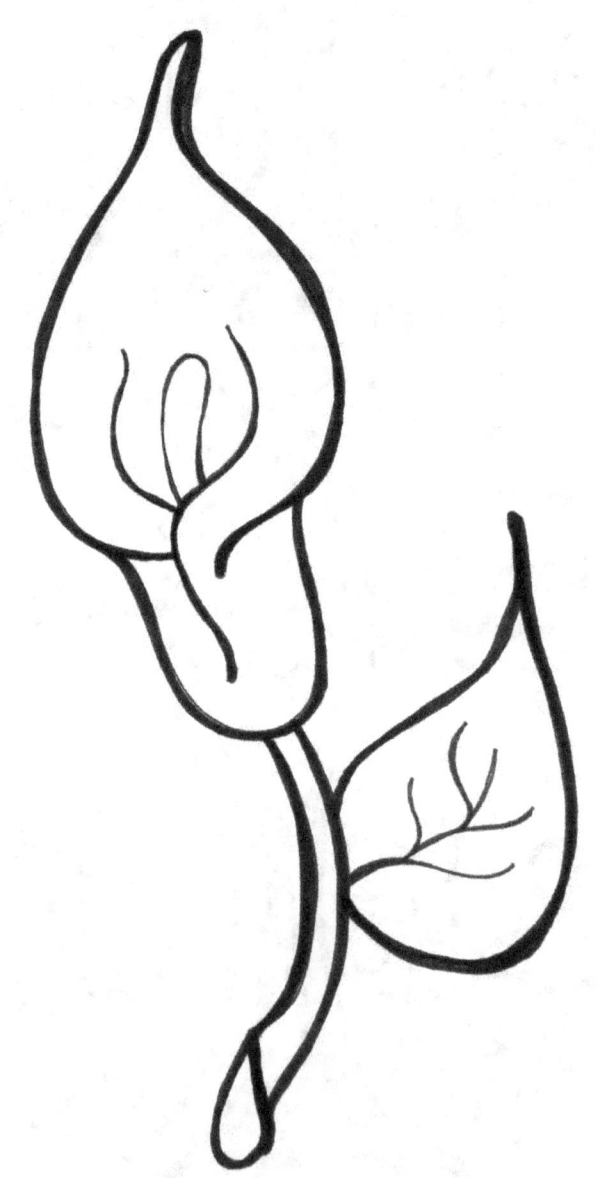

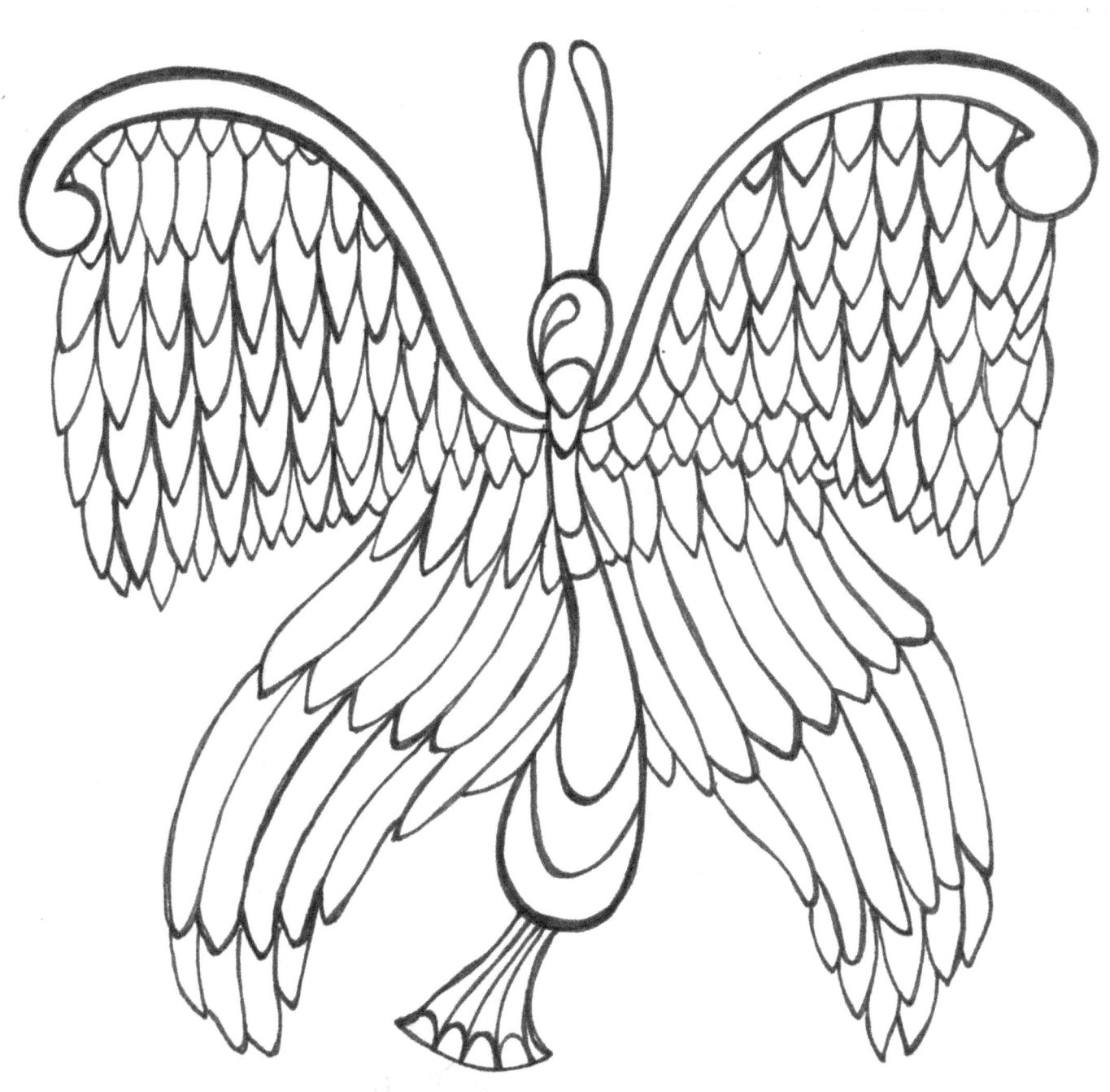

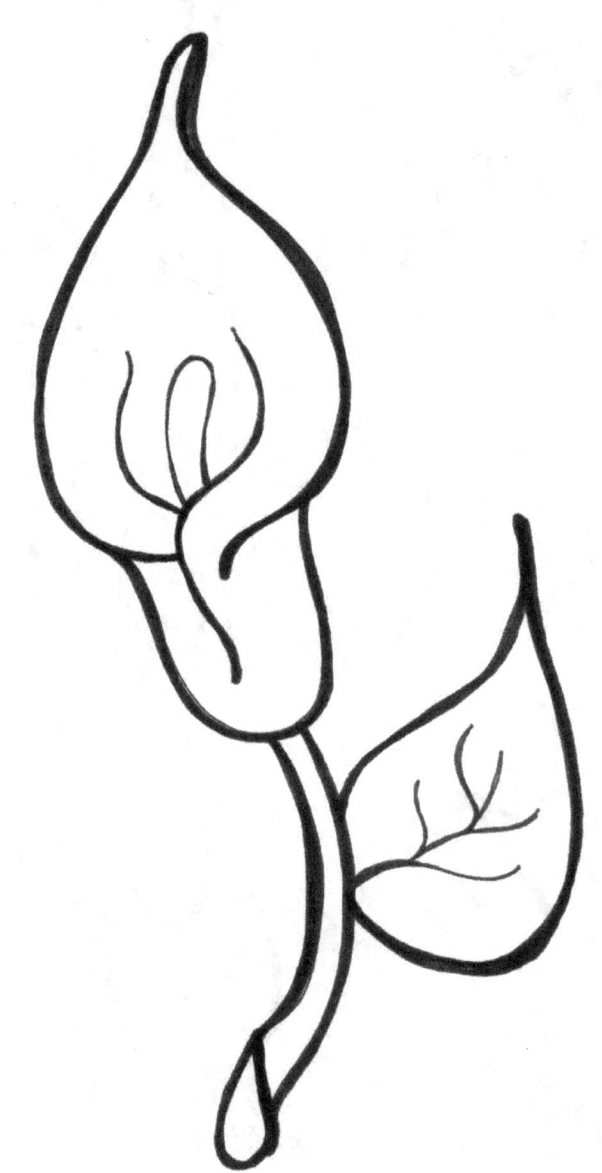

Thank you for adding this coloring book to your collection! Please enjoy these other books by artist Akeem Wayne available on www.akeemwayne.com

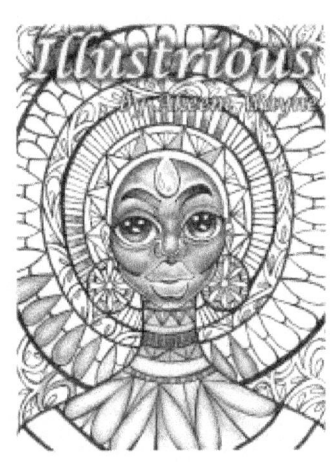
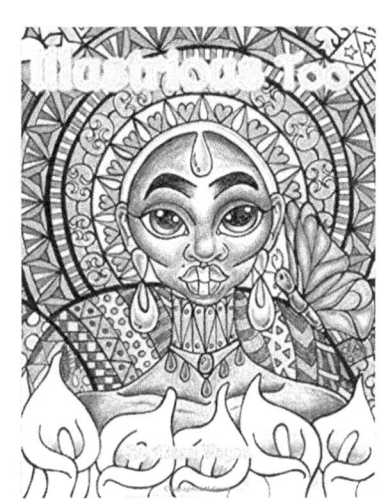

Follow Akeem on Social Media

FB: The Art of Akeem

IG: @artbyakeemwayne

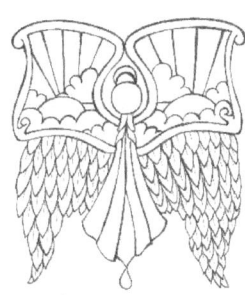